"So many of us are trained to run away from our fears. But what if running toward them is what will actually lead to life? Luke brilliantly weaves together stories and theology in a way that is compelling and beautiful and inspiring for anyone desiring to grow more into the likeness of Jesus day by day."

Jefferson Bethke, *New York Times* bestselling author
of *Jesus > Religion* and *To Hell with the Hustle*

"We all know darkness, but few of us know the gift that exists within the darkness. Luke shows us a way through our fears toward the gift of our truest self in *Befriending Your Monsters*."

Fr. Richard Rohr, author of *Falling Upward*

"*Befriending Your Monsters* helps you see that the darkness you fear might just also be a lifesaving warning. Luke's mixture of humor and wisdom helps you go where you don't want to go, so you can become all that God intends for you."

Ian Morgan Cron, coauthor of *The Road Back to You*

"Fear can steal, but it can also save. This powerful book gave me practical tools to still my knocking knees, thaw my frozen feet, and face the monsters I didn't even realize were lurking under the bed. More than that, it invited me to excavate the unexpected gifts hidden in the dark places where fear often foments. In an age when monsters are multiplying, I can't recommend this book highly enough!"

Jonathan Merritt, contributing writer for *The Atlantic*
and author of *Learning to Speak God from Scratch*

"Thanks to author Luke Norsworthy for giving us a great gift indeed by showing how we can face our fears, overcome the monsters that threaten us, and move forward into a life of virtue and vitality, a deeper, healthier life."

The Most Rev. Michael B. Curry, presiding bishop
and primate, the Episcopal Church

"Occasionally, an author finds a teaching opportunity amid the joys and concerns of a culture that allows for meaningful commentary regarding both what is and what could be. In a time when anxiety is falling on all of us, indiscriminately, and between necessary moments of grace, Luke Norsworthy has found a new and creative way to talk about fear. We need this book and, in particular, his gift for naming faith and its varied expressions as the appropriate antidote for a more holistic approach to our lives."

Suzanne Stabile, author of *The Path Between Us*
and coauthor of *The Road Back to You*

Praise for *God over Good*

"Luke Norsworthy's inviting, accessible, and entirely enjoyable new book is an invitation to come to know God better. Or to come to know God for the first time. Highly recommended."

James Martin, SJ, author of *Jesus: A Pilgrimage*
and *The Jesuit Guide*

"Luke's insight and humor come through his stories and theology in beautifully carved pieces we can savor long after the reading is over. Part memoir, part preaching, part amazing storytelling—it's all a gift offered by a man of great faith who has chosen God over everything. Luke is an exceptional podcaster, pastor, writer, and friend. Read his book."

Becca Stevens, author, priest, and founder of Thistle Farms

Befriending Your Monsters

Befriending Your Monsters

Facing the Darkness of Your Fears to EXPERIENCE the LIGHT

Luke Norsworthy

BakerBooks

a division of Baker Publishing Group
Grand Rapids, Michigan

Published by Baker Books
a division of Baker Publishing Group
PO Box 6287, Grand Rapids, MI 49516-6287
www.bakerbooks.com

Printed in the United States of America

Library of Congress Cataloging-in-Publication Data
Names: Norsworthy, Luke, 1981– author.
Title: Befriending your monsters : facing the darkness of your fears to experience the light / Luke Norsworthy.
Description: Grand Rapids : Baker Books, a division of Baker Publishing Group, 2020. | Includes bibliographical references.
Identifiers: LCCN 2019036302 | ISBN 9780801093333 (paperback)
Subjects: LCSH: Fear—Religious aspects—Christianity.
Classification: LCC BV4908.5 .N67 2020 | DDC 248.8/6—dc23
LC record available at https://lccn.loc.gov/2019036302

Some stories, names, and details have been changed to protect the privacy of the individuals involved.

Published in association with the literary agency of Daniel Literary Group, LLC, Brentwood, TN.

20 21 22 23 24 25 26   7 6 5 4 3 2 1

To my four girls,
with gratitude for showing me the light.

Contents

SECTION III

A Monster-Friendly Life   173

We must abandon the common sense notion that the monsters we meet within ourselves are enemies to be destroyed. Instead, we must cultivate the hope that they can become companions to be embraced, guides to be followed, albeit with caution and respect. *For only our monsters know the way down to that inner place of unity and wholeness; only these creatures of the night know how to travel where there is no light.*

Parker Palmer

Foreword

I STILL CANNOT BELIEVE how much Luke likes sharks. The only panic attack I've had in my life so far came because a fisherman caught a shark and showed it to me. Eyeball to eyeball. Tiny shark mouth jokingly touched to my arm and within seconds, I am panicked. Like block-out-what-just-happened-and-where-I-am kind of panic. Apparently I ran *very* fast on the beach to get away from the tiny shark, but sadly I don't remember it (which is disappointing because I've always wanted to run fast).

I grew up thinking sharks were incredibly dangerous and life-threatening. It's not that I knew it personally; I just saw the same movies you saw and saw the same massive ocean you saw and knew it was too scary.

I read *Befriending Your Monsters* while lying beside a lake, a lake I grew up swimming in and playing around. And yet, sometimes when I jump off the two-story dock and land in the water, I'm scared. I'm scared of what is below me and around me, and I have to do some *major* self-talk not to lose my mind. Of course, there are no sharks in a man-made lake, but there is just no end to the stories my mind will tell me to keep me from doing the thing that is right in front of me.

Just to be clear, there are real things that scare me too. (Not just the idea of saltwater predators in lake water literally hundreds of miles from an ocean.) I'm afraid that my deficits are too much to get over. I'm afraid that if I'm not in control of a situation, it is going to go haywire. I'm afraid my history is going to be too much for someone. I'm afraid I won't survive the losses that some of my friends are experiencing when it is my turn. I'm afraid my prayers aren't going to be answered.

I hear you. You are saying, "Annie, you are afraid God won't answer your prayers the way *you* want them answered. But he always answers." And yes, that would be the correct thing to say. But that's not my fear. My fear is he won't answer.

Luke and his wife and kids have become like family to me. And there is something about being in their house and in their lives that feels really safe. It's not that the scary things go away, but darkness never wins in places full of light.

That's why I read *Befriending Your Monsters* lying by the lake with the sunshine pouring down from the sky over North Georgia. I wanted to remind the darkness that light always wins. I wanted to hear Luke's voice, page after page, a friend of great light in my life, tell me the stories I needed to hear.

There are many things that do not win in your life, if you so choose:

Fear doesn't win.

Pain doesn't win.

Darkness doesn't win.

But it takes choosing light. Choosing to let the light invade the dark corners of your heart, not where things are hidden on purpose but where your courage went to crouch down, thinking this life would be too scary. It's not. Befriend your monsters, let the light in, let your courage stand up, and walk right on into the life you've always wanted.

ANNIE F. DOWNS, bestselling author of *100 Days to Brave* and *Remember God*; host of the *That Sounds Fun* podcast

SECTION I

Meeting Monsters

1

Fake Monsters,
Real Fears

The Song

A TODDLER EMERGES from the dark recesses of our hallway, paci in mouth, pink blankie in hand, and terror furrowing her brow.

"Daddy, I can't sleep. Something skeedy is in my room on the ceiling."

Upon inspection, I realize that I've created this toddler, with ample assistance from my wife; therefore, this crisis is mine to solve.

I spring into action.

As soon as I find the remote.

I'm an empathetic dad, but I'm not reckless. I will pause the TV first.

Three strides carry me from the living room couch to the hallway, where I pick up and begin carrying my daughter back to her room.

I clear my throat, and now I'm ready to sing the song that will expel the fears and put the world back into harmony—"The Monster Song."

I've sung "The Monster Song" to all three of my daughters and at least two coworkers. Each time, it has brought harmony back to the world.

It goes like this:

> There're no monsters in Avery's room.
> There're no monsters in Adalyn's room.
> There're no monsters in Audrey's room.
> So you don't (click sound) have to be scared.

This song obviously brings up some questions. Most notably, why do all my daughters think monsters exist?

If monsters exist in children's minds, then a good night's rest doesn't exist in their adults' reality.

Children know about monsters only because adults tell stories about these nonexistent creatures. Adults could make a pact to remove monster stories for kids and thus increase sleep for adults.

But as adults, we haven't done this, and so we continue to lose out on sleep. Not because we can't get rid of Count Dracula, zombies, or the Big Bad Wolf, but because we can't eradicate what monsters represent. We could set every monster book on fire, but that would not eradicate the real force behind the fictitious fur, flesh, and fangs.

Monstrous Metaphor

MONSTERS HAVE BEEN AROUND for thousands of years. Some believe the Greeks were the first to write about monsters; others believe that long before the Greeks wrote about them, our prehistoric relatives were depicting them. Some think the oldest evidence of a monster is a cave painting dated around 10,000 BC of a half-man, half-beast creature with deerlike antlers and human legs, albeit a human who does lots of squats, called the *Sorcerer of Trois-Frères*. Others, such as Paleolithic art historian André Leroi-Gourhan, say we've found "monstrous forms" in caves from southern France and Spain that are twenty to twenty-five thousand years old.[1]

Our preenlightened ancestors didn't have modern technologies like flashlights, cameras, or Facebook to educate them that half-man and half-deer creatures don't exist. But if it was just ignorance causing them to believe in monsters, why do monsters continue to dominate today's screens?

Because fake monsters embody our real fears.

When the Big Bad Wolf appears with his asthmatic propensity for huffing and puffing, he makes us question the structural integrity of our security.

When an overgrown great white shark develops a humanlike longing for revenge, we feel the need for a bigger boat. The shark's size makes us aware of how small we've always been.

When Godzilla snaps tons of concrete and steel in seconds, we wonder how much strength we possess.

Monsters act as proxies for what truly terrifies us by putting fur, flesh, and fangs on our finitude, our weakness, and our limitation. The gamesmanship might seem excessive, but that doesn't discredit the actual fear.

Fear that I don't matter.

Fear that I don't have enough.

Fear that I don't stack up to those around me.

Fear that I am out of control and in chaos.

The Hebrew Bible speaks of the hippopotamus-like monster, the Behemoth, and the alligator-like monster, the Leviathan. These two monsters often appear in the context of creation as the antagonists to God's creative work. In the first creation account of Genesis, God tamed and separated the chaotic waters of precreation to create a good and orderly world.

> In the beginning when God created the heavens and the earth, the earth was a formless void and darkness covered the face of the deep, while a wind from God swept over the face of the waters. (Gen. 1:1–2)

God overcomes the formless and void water that covers the earth to create our good and ordered world and to create humanity, which isn't just good but very good. Elsewhere, when the Jewish writers describe this anticreation chaos that God overcomes, monsters like the Behemoth and Leviathan replace the water as the chaotic enemy, a common practice in ancient Near Eastern literature. See how Psalm 74 puts fur, flesh, and fangs on the anti-God precreation chaos of the world:

> Yet God my King is from of old,
> > working salvation in the earth.
> You divided the sea by your might;
> > you broke the heads of the dragons in the waters.
> You crushed the heads of Leviathan;
> > you gave him as food for the creatures of the wilderness.
> You cut openings for springs and torrents;
> > you dried up ever-flowing streams.
> Yours is the day, yours also the night;
> > you established the luminaries and the sun. (vv. 12–16)

God brings order out of chaos by dividing the waters, just like in Genesis 1. But here the psalmist adds a second layer of God also conquering the dragons and Leviathan. The most substantial question brought up by this text isn't if these monsters actually exist. The most substantial question is, What real fears do these fake monsters represent?

For the Jewish writers, these monsters might have put scales and teeth on the chaos that an exiled community felt when enslaved miles away from their homeland. The fear that their oppressors (and thus their oppressors' gods) had more power than their God. The fear that they were small, powerless, and out of control.

The psalmist expresses the common attitude about monsters found outside of Judaism. Anthropologist David Gilmore writes:

The monster is a metaphor for all that must be repudiated by the human spirit. It embodies the existential threat to social life, the chaos, atavism, and negativism that symbolize destructiveness and all other obstacles to order and progress, all that which defeats, destroys, draws back, undermines, subverts the human project.[2]

Your monster is the metaphor or the proxy for what prevents you from becoming what you were created to be. You were created not just good but very good; yet disordering and distorting forces pull against and subvert your Creator's best intentions for you. To live this good life, you can't continue to run away scared. You must turn around and go back into the dark, so you can experience the light.

Monster Fuel

WE CAN'T RID OURSELVES OF MONSTERS because today there still is an endless supply of what monsters represent:

Fear.

Anthropologist Alex Bentley and his researchers analyzed the emotional content of millions of twentieth-century books, ranging from writings with overt emotional content, like novels or books on current events, to books without clear emotional content, like technical manuals, automotive repair guides, and literature written by accountants. Bentley found the existence of an emotional difference among the decades as seen by the most used emotional words.[3]

The 1920s lived into their moniker of the Roaring 20s in that they contained the peak of joy-related words.

The 1940s were a time of great sadness, with the nadir being 1941, the year the United States entered World War II.

Over the last century, the usage of words expressing basic feelings such as joy, anger, and disgust all declined. Compared to the past one hundred years, today we are less expressive of all emotions but one: fear.

Our church often fills out prayer cards during the service. Without fail, there is always one major theme from the prayer cards—fear.

Fear of finances.

Fear of the future.

Fear of not being enough.

Fear of not having enough.

Fear for their kids' well-being.

Fear of never being able to move on from the past.

The Rev. Adam Hamilton did a bit more precise study of his congregation's relationship with fear. Of the twenty-four hundred parishioners he surveyed, 85 percent had either moderate or significant levels of fear.[4]

Fear and all its presentations surround us.

We fear failure.

We fear the future.

We fear what's next.

We fear the diagnosis.

We fear being exposed as an impostor.

We fear that we are failures and that our lives are meaningless.

We even fear expressing our fear.

Hamilton writes:

> I've noticed that men are often hesitant to admit that they feel fearful because it seems to be a sign of weakness. Instead, we talk about being "stressed." But if you poke around our stress a bit to look for what's driving us, you'll find worry and anxiety—sometimes outright panic.[5]

Our culture capitalizes on fear. The news networks know that terror turns on televisions. If it bleeds (metaphorically or literally), it leads in ratings and clicks. Fear grabs attention and gets us to grab products.

In a Duracell battery commercial, a mom plays with her boy in a picturesque park on a perfect day, only to be interrupted by the ominous voice of Jeff Bridges saying, "It was a beautiful day at the park. That turned to panic in an instant."

The child slips off-screen and terror covers the mother's face.

And then, back comes Jeff Bridges's voice, "And everything depended on a Brickhouse child locator. Packed inside every locator is the only battery Brickhouse trusts—Duracell."

That bothersome-enough tableau doesn't satiate Duracell, so into the frame rolls a creepy, windowless white van.

And we all know what a windowless van at a park with a missing boy insinuates.

And Duracell knows that if we have enough fear, they will always sell enough batteries.

Fear is all around us, so is it any wonder that we still have monsters?

Something has to put fur, flesh, and fangs on all that fear.

Too Dark

THESE DAYS, MY WIFE, Lindsay, spends many late nights as the only one awake in our house. She calls it being the "queen of the night." That's not to be confused with being a "lady of the night," which has the same hours but much different responsibilities. While I go to bed early, she stays up late. But it hasn't always been this way.

A decade and a half ago, we had moved to Florida for my first job out of seminary. During that season, Lindsay went to bed early because she was working the day shift as a nurse in the neonatal intensive care unit while also growing our first child in her womb. I stayed up late because I had nowhere to go the next day.

After television had adequately numbed my mind, I would sneak back into a pitch-black bedroom, the darkness courtesy of a remnant from years before when Lindsay worked the night shift—blackout curtains.

On the good nights, I fell directly asleep.

Other nights, the darkness would keep me awake.

On this night, the darkness got the best of me.

The stillness allowed the words I had tried to ignore to come to life. Dizzying words that brought more darkness into the room.

Luke, you aren't good enough.

Luke, you are a loser who can't provide for his family.

Back in college, a friend who enjoyed his and my share of alcohol told me that when his inebriation caused him to feel like the room was spinning, he would put a foot on the ground to steady himself. I'm not sure why I remembered that piece of information, but in this moment the advice seemed helpful. So I slid my left foot onto the ground, but the room kept spinning. To be clear, it wasn't spinning because of being in a bar that night. It was from an elders' meeting two months before.

Wednesday nights at that church began with a church-wide meeting meal, and then the church's elders and ministers would meet. If you don't know what elders are, think board members—that is, my bosses.

During the meal, I sat next to an elder, Sal, whose grandson was on my flag football team. We had a game that evening, two hours after our meeting. I asked Sal if he thought we would be done in time for me to make the game.

He said, "Uh . . . I think you will be out in time."

By the time I made my way from the fellowship hall to the conference room on the other side of the building, all six elders had made it into the room and to their seats, a surprising feat for men who were, on average, four decades older than me. These six elders weren't the elders who had hired me as a twenty-four-year-old fresh out of seminary. Those elders had all resigned amid a scandal six months after I arrived. After the scandal, the church of two hundred picked this new group to run the congregation.

After I took my seat, one of the new elders slid a document across the table to me. A second elder began reading it aloud. I silently read the document in a fraction of the time it took for the elder to read it. In the lag time before he caught up, all I could think was,

Sal was right, you are going to be out in time for your game.

My elementary school in Philadelphia required students to wear either blue or gray pants. I once wore a pair of dark green pants, thinking that supporting my Irish heritage trumped the dress code.

The principal didn't support my Irish pride.

As my class stood in the hallway in a line, the principal walked by and without slowing his gait said, "Luke, come to my office."

On that day, the principal was no pal.

Once in his office, I dialed home to tell my mother of my unpalatable transgression.

My eyes welled with tears, and my throat closed up, leaving the only sound for my mother to hear on the other end of the phone was her son's whimpering.

As a kid, I didn't know what to call that feeling in the principal's office. When I felt it again fifteen years later in that elders' meeting, I had the word to describe it.

Shame.

Shame slides on like an unwieldy backpack, slumping shoulders and constricting lungs. At first, you fight to keep your head up, but the weight and your newfound aversion to eye contact win. As Brené Brown tells us, there's a difference between guilt and shame. Guilt says there's something wrong with what I've done. Shame says there's something wrong with who I am.[6] No matter the words on the page that the elders handed me, I felt something was wrong with me.

The document said the church couldn't afford to pay me after the previous year's substantial financial downturn; therefore, I needed to find new employment. They assumed I would quickly find new employment without causing harm to me, my wife, or the unborn child whom I had just announced to the church three days before in my sermon.

No one said I was fired, but it sure felt like a firing.

I didn't know what to do next, but I did know that I didn't want Lindsay to feel the way I did. So I went to the flag football game.

Surprisingly, I don't remember if we won or lost that game, but I do remember sitting alone on the bench, staring up at the scoreboard while praying that the game would never end. As the clock ticked down to straight zeros, I had a flashback to one of the final scenes in the college football movie from the '90s, *The Program*. Senior linebacker Steve Lattimer sat on the bench as the last seconds of his final football game ticked away. His head hung low, tears smearing the Native American–inspired war paint that covered his face. Lattimer's coach had confronted him earlier in the game about his obvious steroid abuse. When the game ended, Lattimer would have to face the consequences for his drug abuse. Lattimer wished the clock would miraculously stop, so he could stay in the fantasy world of sports. I felt just like Lattimer.

Well,

minus the steroids,

the face paint,

and the actual tears.

When the game ended, I left my fantasy world and finally told Lindsay. And despite how well she handled it, the nightmare became real.

That night I didn't just lose a job; I lost part of myself.

I lost my sense of invincibility that I could be the master of my own fate.

I lost my sense of control that I could keep chaos away from me.

Months later, on one of those nights when I finally did fall asleep, I had a dream of a snake slithering up our sidewalk toward the front door of our Florida home. In this dream, I step outside, grab the snake, and kill it. I leave the snake's dead body on the sidewalk, which seemed like the right thing to do since it was Florida. Then I go back inside.

A few minutes later, I look through the same window to see the same snake alive and again slithering closer toward our house. So

I go outside and kill it. And again, I leave the dead snake on the sidewalk.

I go back in the house and look out the window to again see the snake slither toward the front door. This process repeats itself over and over again in the dream until I am wide awake in my bed, wishing our blackout curtains weren't so competent at keeping out all the light.

Certainly, the six garter snakes found in our flower beds during a spring cleaning day weeks before influenced the dream.

But maybe,

just maybe,

the dream wasn't only the random coincidence of my subconscious cycling through recent memories.

Maybe the zombie snake put scales on the chaos all around me.

Maybe the zombie snake put fangs on the fear that I couldn't keep adversity away from my home or the fear that all my efforts to control my circumstances by getting the *right* degrees, the *right* résumé, and the *right* experience so I would have the *right* life were impotent.

Maybe the snake embodied the fear that something is wrong with me, because if that church thinks they are better off without me, what does that say about me?

Losing my job didn't create those issues; it only revealed the issues that I had given my best effort to hide. It didn't cause me to find my meaning in my occupational performance, nor did it make me arrogantly assume I was in control of my life. It only revealed the monsters that had always resided within my heart.

Often adversity doesn't create; it only reveals what has been there all along.

The substantial question then becomes, What do we do when our monsters are revealed?

Options

LET'S GO BACK TO THAT MOMENT from your childhood when you thought you heard a monster in your room. I'm sure you can remember one of those moments.

Ten minutes before, you had put on your favorite pajamas and lay down in your darkened room. Now, your eyelids are heavy and the trailers for your dreams have begun playing when a sound from your closet startles you.

Your eyelids fly open. Your heart rate surpasses the boiling point.

It sounded like a claw scratching the inside of the closet door, but you aren't sure.

So you get really still, hoping to get a better understanding of the sound, while also hoping to never hear it again.

You wait.

And wait.

It seems like forever.

But in actuality it's been only thirty seconds.

Just as you've convinced yourself that what you heard was a figment of your imagination and your heart rate descends to a livable level, it happens again.

You can't talk yourself out of this one. So what do you do?

Option one: you stay statue-like under the covers in the hopes that the monster waiting to emerge from your closet will overlook you and leave your room. You spend the rest of the night living in this heart-about-to-burst-out-of-your-chest feeling until daylight rescues you or you pass out.

Option two: you grab your flashlight in one hand and your light saber in the other. You stuff a pillow under your shirt for protection, and then you make your way across the darkened room to face the monster.

Two options: hide or confront.

As we age, the options don't change.

Adults replace burrowing under blankets with more refined hiding tactics like occupational obsessions, striving for social standing, vicarious living through children, or the numbness brought on by preferred vices such as wine, chocolate, or social media. They aren't as warm and cuddly as your beloved blanket, but they are just as ineffective.

If we never face our fears, we will always be haunted by them.

If we don't confront our shame, shame will always dictate our identity.

If we never befriend our monster, we will always be enslaved by our monster.

And this might just be the reason we tell children monster stories. Maybe we accept our children having a few nightmares because they learn that only one viable option exists when a monster appears. As has been said:

> Fairy tales don't teach kids that monsters exist.
> They teach kids that monsters can be defeated.[7]

Only one good option exists when it comes to fear: you must go where you don't want to go, so you can become who you were created to be.

When the scary monster abducts the hero's child and takes the child back into its deep, dark cave, our hero goes into the cave to get her child back. When the fictionalized man-eating shark keeps eating kids, the chief of police, who of course is afraid of water, gets on a boat and heads into the water to fight the monster.

Monsters force us into the places we don't want to go because you can't find the salvation you need unless you embrace the darkness you fear.

When shame, weakness, insecurity, vulnerability, or doubt appear, we don't find salvation by hiding from them. We find salvation by befriending them.

I hope you learn in the following pages how your greatest fear might just be your greatest teacher. What might be the worst thing you've ever experienced, like getting fired, might be one of the greatest gifts you'll ever receive. In the beginning, humanity was created full of divine goodness, and the Creator's intention for you today is to live out of that goodness. To live fully out of love, courage, wholehearted-ness, and gratitude and not out of fear, discouragement, isolation, or entitlement. But this way of life doesn't come without intentionality. To receive the grace of your Creator's intention for you, I invite you to take what feels like a counterintuitive journey, because for you to become who you were created to be, you usually have to go where you never wanted to be.

There's a reason this book isn't titled *Eradicating the Monsters*, because what you aren't going to learn in this book is how to get rid of them.

A small emergency room in my neighborhood was in the last stages of construction—roof complete, lights on, parking lot paved and painted—when the builders hung a peculiar tarp over the building's sign. Maybe because if you need life-and-death help, the last thing you need to see is a sign promoting an emergency room that isn't operational. If you've purchased this book hoping it will surgically remove all fear from your life, you will be like the person showing up to the inoperative emergency room. So let this disclaimer function like the tarp over the sign. Not because the book is incomplete, but because that expectation is unrealistic. The overwhelming majority of us will never eradicate our monsters, but we can befriend them. We can learn not only to accept their perpetual presence but also to see how they can be the catalyst for us becoming all that we were created to be. And anything that does that, no matter how you first meet it or what it sounds like, is a friend to you, because nothing is more important than living into the goodness of what your Creator designed you to be.

You aren't going to find a plan to eradicate your monsters in this book, but here's what you will find. The first section of the book will tell you where you have to go to find your monster and what you will find when you get there. The second section of the book discusses the three universal monsters: comparison, more, and success. Using a four-part template from the story of a Jewish prophet named Jonah, I will show you how to befriend the three universal monsters. In the third section of the book, we will discuss how (not) to live a monster-friendly life.

But first.

Let's go back to the toddler who emerged from the dark hallway . . .

Seconds before, my three-year-old daughter had run around the corner, pink blankie in hand and terror on her brow.

Now, with her safely deposited in my arms and comforted by my singing, I carry her into her darkened room and ask her to show me the monster.

She points at a blinking red light on her ceiling, exclaiming, "There's the skeedy monster."

"And that's the skeedy monster's eye!"

The skeedy (scary) monster's eye was surrounded by a five-inch white circle, which I knew not to be the eye socket of a monster, because I had recently installed that five-inch white circle on her ceiling. What appeared to be the terrifying red eye of a dragon, waiting to consume her, was actually a light from a smoke detector intended to warn her of danger and keep her alive. The monster was a warning, not intended to hurt, but to save. The English word *monster* actually comes from the Latin word *monere*, which means "to warn."[8]

Your monsters might just be the same thing to you: a warning.

Not to hurt you,

but to save you.

2

Into the Dark

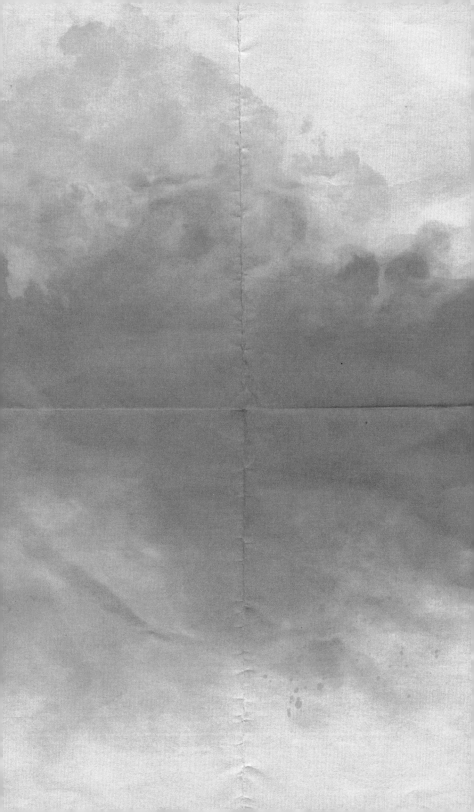

Darkness

OUR OLDEST DAUGHTER climbed out of her crib at fifteen months. The first solution to this problem was to put a lid on her crib. Upon further consideration, we concluded that asking our child to sleep in a crib with a lid seemed to be a parenting move that would cost her an extra six months in counseling, because a crib with a lid could also be called a cage. Instead, we opted to give her a big-girl bed. Four minutes into the first night with the big-girl bed, she began sneaking into the living room.

There is no nice way to say what I did next.

So I will just say it as though it was my wife's fault.

What my wife did next was to begin locking our daughter in her room.

Technically, it wasn't a lock, but rather a doorknob that toddler fingers couldn't open. Which is like when the Honda salesman told me that I would grow to love having a minivan. Both deceitful statements cause someone to be imprisoned where they don't want to be.

Yet locking her in her room was the best option.

For me.

She didn't concur. Every night she laid down on the floor right next to the door.

Not near the door, but right up next to the door.

I found this out the hard way.

You never forget the first time you open a door and hit your daughter's head. Luckily, she did.

Assuming one almost-concussion to be enough, the next time I entered her room at night, I first assessed her location by lying down on the hallway floor to look through the space between the bottom of the door and the carpet.

What I saw was a fifteen-month-old's eye staring directly back at me from the other side of the door.

Despite having a door hit her in the face once already, she still preferred laying face against the door in harm's way to being safely in her bed.

Lindsay went to Target that evening and solved this crisis with the purchase of a nightlight.

With the faint glow of a tiny pink light, she no longer slept on the floor. Turns out that our daughter didn't hate her crib or her big-girl bed. She hated being in the dark alone.

She's not the only one. Most of us do whatever we can to avoid the feeling of being alone in the dark. As Blaise Pascal said, "All of humanity's problems stem from man's inability to sit quietly in a room alone."[1]

For a behavioral study, college students entered a room, knowing they would be there alone for twenty minutes with nothing but a device that could shock them. Before the experiment began, participants received a single shock from the device, informing them of the unpleasant sting they would feel if they pressed the button over the next twenty minutes. Despite experiencing the device's pain, one-third of female participants and two-thirds of male participants shocked themselves during the test. One participant used the device every six seconds for the entire twenty minutes for a total of 190 shocks.[2]

Roughly half of the participants preferred the negative feeling of a shock to the feeling of sitting quietly in a room alone. Maybe because the participants, just like the rest of us, don't want to deal with what comes up when the noise and distractions go down. Maybe we don't like to experience the darkness of silence because that's when the monsters appear.

There's a reason why we don't want to sit quietly alone.

In silence, the worries from which our busyness has distanced us finally catch up to us.

In darkness, the monsters we've pushed under our beds come back out.

In solitude, with the absence of distractions, the critical voices inside our heads commandeer our undivided attention.

In stillness, there's nowhere to go.

Darkness, at least how I'm using it in this book, is not an actual ominous place within the world but a metaphor for the vulnerable place within you. It's not actually a cave or a dark forest; it's where your tricks and techniques for making yourself feel like you've got it all figured out no longer work. It's the part of you that you don't want anyone to see, because you feel that if they knew that facet of you, they would probably never again want to see any of you.

When I say darkness, I'm referring to the place where the light shines brightest on your greatest insecurities and failures.

Where the brightness of your personality no longer covers your anxieties.

Where you no longer have the faculties and the agency to mask your weaknesses.

Where you stop pretending to be what you do and instead have to take inventory of what you've actually become.

Where you can't focus on what you will do to make it right but instead have to exist within the consequences of what you've done wrong.

This is why we don't want to go into the darkness.

But don't shame yourself. Even Jesus wasn't thrilled about entering into the darkness. In Matthew's account of the night before the crucifixion, Jesus goes off to pray with his twelve disciples at the garden of Gethsemane, which literally means "oil press." A fitting name, since it's near the Mount of Olives and is the place where the powers and principalities of this world pressed in on Jesus until life was squeezed out of him.

Jesus withdraws from the Twelve to a more remote place in the garden but not without bringing his inner circle, Peter, James, and John. Even Jesus doesn't want to sit quietly alone. A grief-stricken and agitated Jesus begs his three friends to stay awake while he prays, in effect, "My Father, I don't want this to happen. If there's any other way, let it be. But if not, I will go where you want me to go."

Jesus returns to find his closest friends with closed eyes. "Guys, I'm only asking you to stay awake for just one hour!"

Then Jesus goes off a second time to pray the same prayer, only to return to the same disciples in the same soporific state.

Then a third time—same prayer, same sleeping disciples, same disappointment. Their spirit was willing, but their flesh was weak.

Jesus knew just how weak their flesh was going to be, but still Jesus invited them to be with him. Jesus chose the sting of disappointment over the shocking pain of being alone in the darkness.

Monomyth

ONCE UPON A TIME IN A LAND FAR, far away, a fire-breathing dragon lived inside a cave high up on a mountain. Every evening, the dragon's thunderous roar filled the valley below, and its fire lit the sky above. The villagers down in the valley kept their heads bowed and their lips sealed because they thought if the dragon never saw their eyes or heard their words, then maybe,

just maybe,

the dragon would let them live in peace down below in their separate world. Like a colony of ants, the villagers at the bottom of the valley were always working but never making a sound.

One day, a young orphan stumbled into the village, dirty and hungry. The kind villagers had pity on the boy's lonely plight. They adopted him as one of their own. The village's elders, Patrice and Winslow, declared the child to be one of them. He wasn't anyone's child in particular; he was everyone's child. The fearful villagers couldn't leave the valley to look for food or water, so they survived on the meager sustenance the valley provided. But what they had, they shared with the orphan boy. Every night a different family in the village opened their home, giving him a little bit of food and a warm place to sleep. Nurtured by the villagers' love, the boy grew with a belly that never was too full, but with a heart that always had an excess of bravery.

Let's stop the story right there. How is this story going to end?

We all know that somehow, someway the orphan boy, the villagers, and the dragon will end up face-to-face. Because we all know one thing about monsters: they never stay hidden.

Monsters lurk in the shadows of the darkest cave atop the highest mountain. They swim twenty thousand leagues below. They hide underneath your bed or in the back of your closet. Monsters exist in what experimental psychologist Richard Beck calls *epistemic limits*.[3] These are the places that are hard to know and even harder to want to know.

Yet it's into this darkness that monsters invite us, not for our demise but for our salvation. This story gets told over and over again.

The Jewish prophet Jonah hated the Assyrians who had conquered his people. So where does God call Jonah to go? The Assyrian capital, Nineveh.

In the animated film *Trolls*, Justin Timberlake's character, Branch, hates to sing because singing brings up the memory of losing his grandmother. So, of course, for Branch to save his friends, he must sing.

While Scripture doesn't say much about what Jesus did between his death and resurrection,[4] the Apostles' Creed states that Jesus didn't experience just the worst of the world but also the worst of the age to come—hell.

> Who was conceived by the Holy Spirit,
> born of the virgin Mary,
> suffered under Pontius Pilate,
> was crucified, died, and was buried;
> *he descended to hell*;
> on the third day he rose again from the dead;
> he ascended to heaven,
> and is seated at the right hand of God the Father almighty;
> from there he will come to judge the living and the dead.[5]

Jesus goes into the darkness of death to extend salvation to the whole world.

Mythologist Joseph Campbell refers to this narrative template as the Hero's Journey or the Monomyth.[6] The hero is called to adventure, to enter the unknown, where the hero faces challenges and is transformed. The hero overcomes the enemy. Then the hero returns home, forever changed by the experience.

Monsters invite us to go where we don't want to go so that we can become everything we were intended to be. The invitation into the dark recesses of our hearts and souls—to engage the fears, insecurities, and self-doubt—is an invitation no one wants but everyone needs so that we can live into our Creator's intention for us.

The Rest of the Story

OKAY, SO BACK TO THE STORY of the villagers, the dragon, and the orphan.

Years have passed, and the orphan boy has grown in wisdom and in stature. He appears to be like every other quiet villager, except he doesn't cower with every roar coming from the mountaintop. He alone sneaks glances at the mountaintop with its berry-covered bushes, crystal-clear lake, and frolicking deer and rabbits.

One morning, he's gone.

Just gone.

The village breaks into a panic. Hushed whispers of his name fill the valley. Every nook and cranny are searched. Just as quietly as the orphan boy had stumbled into the town years prior, the orphan man has now disappeared.

"Up there!" a young boy screams.

The village gasps in unison as the scream breaks the village's silence, and then a second gasp occurs when they see the outline of a person, their person, summiting the mountain.

"We must do something!" the elder Patrice says.

"But we can't go up there," Winslow says to his fellow elder.

"Winslow, we can't do nothing."

"But Patrice, if we go, we will all die."

"If we do nothing, then our hearts will have already died."

Acquiescing to his fellow elder, Winslow, with Patrice by his side, leads the villagers up the mountain.

On top of the mountain, the orphan man lets out childish giggles as he plucks berries, drinks the lake's crystal-clear water, and chases rabbits. The sounds of delight wake the normally nocturnal dragon. In a groggy stupor, it steps out of the cave to see the orphan swimming in its lake. The dragon lets out a roar.

The man's glee vanishes, and the crystal-clear lake turns a slightly yellower hue.

The dragon, always one to toy with its food, stalks the man around the lake, taking its time, until the dragon has cornered him at the mouth of its cave. The orphan man is trapped, yet he will not cower. He picks up two stones from inside the cave. The first flies out of his hand, hitting the dragon's nose but not affecting the dragon at all. He throws the second stone, but he doesn't see where it lands.

He never felt the dragon's fireball that took his life. It emerged from the dragon's nostrils too hot and too fast.

But it was seen by the villagers who look down upon their beloved's demise from the top of the cave. Empowered by their anger, in unison the villagers push a cottage-size boulder off the top of the cave. It fell directly on the dragon below.

The dragon never made another sound.

On that day, the two rocks the orphan man threw did no damage to the dragon, but the legend that grew from that day forward told a different story. The villagers honored him with a yearly festival on the day of his death when Patrice and Winslow would retell the story of his battle against the dragon that gave the community the ability to resettle atop the mountain where they now lived without fear or scarcity.

Developed in the Dark

AS THE LINE OFTEN ATTRIBUTED to Ernest Hemingway goes, "There is nothing to writing. All you do is sit down at a typewriter and bleed." Writing, at least the life-giving kind, doesn't come from comfort but from self-sacrifice. Good art always costs the artist something, whether it be their dignity, their secrets, their hopes, or part of their humanity.

All of us have a gift to give the world that will cost us something. The price of that gift is your entrance into your darkness because that's where you are developed into who the world needs you to be. My mother turned a room in my childhood home into her photography room. Drying papers hung from a clothesline, trays with chemicals sat waiting for paper to be dipped in them, and not a glimmer of light was visible. For the pictures to become what they were intended to be, they required darkness. Like my mom's pictures, our soul requires darkness to develop. Our attractive exterior armor shines in the light, but our soul is formed in the dark.

Barbara Brown Taylor tells a story of going spelunking in the mountains of West Virginia in *Learning to Walk in the Dark*. While in one of the darkest parts of the cave, she found a beautiful rock that glimmered in the minuscule light emerging from her flashlight. Barbara picked up the beautiful rock and brought it back with her. Once out of the cave, the rock no longer looked beautiful. The sunlight muted the rock's beauty, revealing it to be a regular piece of gravel. It was only in the darkness that she could see its true beauty.

She goes on to write this about the darkness:

> I have learned things in the dark that I could never have learned in
> the light, things that have saved my life over and over again, so that
> there is really only one logical conclusion. I need darkness as much
> as I need light.[7]

She's not the only one who needs the darkness in order to develop.

In Matthew's Gospel, after Jesus emerges from the waters of his baptism, the heavens open and a voice declares, "This is my Son, the Beloved, with whom I am well pleased" (Matt. 3:17).

Afterward, the Spirit leads Jesus into the wilderness where Jesus fasts alone for forty days, and then the devil tempts him. It's almost as if, at Jesus's baptism, he's named the Beloved Son, then through the isolation, hunger, and temptation of the wilderness, he's formed into being the Beloved Son.*

It's in the darkness of his wilderness experience that something happens to Jesus. And it's in the darkness that covered the earth when Jesus hung on the cross and died that something happens to all of us. Christians call that day Good Friday because Christianity has historically understood the benefit of the dark.

The basic recipe for any story is the simple mixture of conflict and a character whom the audience cares about, whether that concern be for their success or failure. Under pressure, some characters break badly, becoming a mere shell of their Creator's intentions. Others become the best version of themselves. Good stories teach us what many parents forget: the worst thing for a child isn't experiencing adversity; the worst thing is being unable to grow. Too often, parents

---

*If the idea of Jesus's formation is problematic for you, please see Luke 2:52: "And Jesus grew in wisdom and stature, and in favor with God and man" (NIV). According to Luke's Gospel, Jesus clearly experienced growth or formation.

aim to keep their children happy. The parent swoops in at the first appearance of adversity to "save the day," but in doing so they shortcut their child's ability to grow through struggles. If you want your kids to always be happy, eradicate adversity. If you want your kids to be good, teach them to navigate adversity.

Christianity has known for thousands of years what Joseph Campbell's Hero's Journey has recently been trying to teach us. Adversity is required for growth. James, the brother of Jesus, writes these peculiarly positive words about adversity:

> My brothers and sisters, whenever you face trials of any kind, consider
> it nothing but joy, because you know that the testing of your faith
> produces endurance; and let endurance have its full effect, so that you
> may be mature and complete, lacking in nothing. (James 1:2–4)

Our character can't be formed, our resilience can't be strengthened, our central values can't be defined, and our truest self can't emerge unless we go into the darkness.

Confession

AS A MIDDLE SCHOOLER, I expected every church service to follow the same routine. The sermon ends with an obligatory and unaccepted invitation for anyone needing to confess sins to come forward to the front row. We all sing the invitation song, hear a closing prayer, then leave to go eat. Like Pavlov's dogs, the invitation song cued my stomach that it was time for food.

But one time someone did accept the invitation. And I will never forget it.

Rattled by the uncustomary behavior and my delayed meal, my eyes couldn't stop staring at the man sitting in the front row while the rest of the congregation continued singing.

The preacher joined him on the front pew and quietly conversed with him while we finished the song. After we sat down, the gentleman stepped up on the stage, walked behind the pulpit, and pulled out a written statement. I don't remember what the note said, but I do remember what happened after he concluded.

He walked down from the stage and stood by the preacher.

Then the entire congregation formed a line, and one after another we walked up to the man and shook his hand. He had obviously done something very ugly, but what the church did was beautiful. Hundreds walked by embracing him and welcoming the man despite his transgression.

But it must have been awful for him.

Can you imagine facing four hundred people from your church, one at a time, as they look you in the eye after you've confessed something so bad you had to read it off a prewritten note?

I imagine the only thing worse for him than making a huge spectacle in front of his church would have been to keep his shame monster hidden away in the darkness.

In the darkness, shame, doubt, worry, and self-hatred flourish. When fears remain isolated, they have power and dominion over us, but when we acknowledge and confront them, we gain power over them. Just as Adam in the second creation story in Genesis names the animals because the animals were subordinate to him, our naming of our own monsters begins the process of us gaining dominion over them.

Monsters that have been named are monsters that can be defanged. As Carl Jung said, "Until you make the unconscious conscious, it will direct your life and you will call it fate."[8]

For Jonah, it cost him having his heart revealed for what it was: anti-God.

For the villagers facing the dragon atop the mountain, it cost them one of their own.

For the man from my childhood church to face his monster, it cost him his pride and reputation.

For you to become who you were created to be, it will also come at a price.

Usher

SPEAKING OF CONFESSION, let me tell you about the one time I went into a nightclub.

I went once or twice to nightclubs (or the closest thing that Abilene, Texas, has to a nightclub) when I was in college but not to see what was happening inside. Instead, it was to "witness" to people outside the clubs. And by witness, I mean shoving into their hands pieces of paper warning the club attendees of the fires of hell. This also served as a field sobriety test, because they shouldn't be driving a car if they were not sober enough to evade the Bible thumpers. On a side note, I still can't imagine why none of those people ever came to a church service with me.

Fast-forward a decade, and I'm now on the inside.

It was the wedding weekend of a friend who had asked me to officiate the service. The wedding party was going out to a nightclub, and I didn't want to be the judgmental preacher who abstained from associating with the heathens. If Jesus spent so much time with people drinking that he was confused for an alcoholic, I figured I could venture into a nightclub one time.

We walked up to a bouncer, after cutting in front of the line of people behind a red-velvet rope. Someone in our group did that cool thing where people shake hands while secretly exchanging money. The bouncer slid his thirty pieces of silver into his pocket, unclipped the red-velvet rope, and opened the door for us. We proceeded down a darkened staircase. I could feel the music reverberating and my eternal security sinking.

We turned the corner at the bottom of the staircase and were in the nightclub. I immediately felt like I had entered an Usher music video. For the next hour, I stood awkwardly close to my friends to avoid my greatest fear: a dance battle.

Miraculously, I survived the rest of the night without being thrust into the center of a circle of angsty club-goers settling their conflicts with dance moves.

The DJ announced that the night was ending and the club was shutting down in a few minutes. Despite the ample instruction and my complete dad move of humming Semisonic's "Closing Time," no one was leaving. Turns out that club-goers after the last song of the night are similar to churchgoers in the lobby during the first song of the morning. Neither of them move until drastic measures are taken. In the club-goers case, the drastic measure was the lights.

The Usher-music-video lights were replaced with halogen lights. And as halogen lights always do, they made everyone look like a zombie. The club invested much into making life appear sexier and cooler with minimal lighting that hid reality, but when the halogen lights sobered up the room, no one wanted to stay. The club's vibe depended on the darkness. When the lights came on, reality rushed in, and everyone went out.

"We are only as sick as our secrets," says the Alcoholics Anonymous mantra.

Addictions live in the darkness where deception flourishes. In the darkness, shallow attempts to mask our loneliness with momentary relationships seem great. But when the light appears, our attempts are revealed to be the very choices that drive us into more isolation and despair.

In the darkness, the lies we tell ourselves feel true. They thrive in isolation. For our health, we must go into the darkness, acknowledge the lies, and name them, because that's how we illuminate them.

By naming the tendency to determine your value based on sizing yourself up to friends or enemies, you illuminate the lies of the Monster of Comparison so you can see who you truly are.

By noting the presence within you of the insatiable appetite of the Monster of More that steals away your gratitude, you put light on the darkness so the darkness will not overcome you.

By acknowledging the voice that says you are what you do, the light can set you free from the Monster of Success to be defined by something more substantive than achievements and appearances.

Cows or Buffalo

I'VE BEEN TOLD that when big thunderstorms come in from the west and roll eastward through the great plains of eastern Colorado, cows and buffalo respond differently.

As cows sense a storm coming in from the west, they run away from the storm and toward the east. The storm will eventually catch up to the cows because, well, they are cows. As the edge of the storm begins to pelt them with raindrops, they continue running eastward. This means that now, unbeknownst to the cows, they are running with the storm. The cows' attempt to flee the storm prolongs their suffering.

Buffalo don't.

Buffalo wait for the storm to peak over the crest of the mountain, and when feeling the edge of the storm, they too begin to run, but not eastward like cows. The buffalo run westward, directly into the storm. Running through the storm minimizes the suffering they endure. They still feel the rain and the wind, but they get through it quicker.

Much like cows, we run and run, prolonging our discomfort. We hide under the blankets instead of going to confront the sound in the closet. We numb ourselves with productivity, success, pleasure, and endless digital distractions and never take inventory of the darkness within us. We run away because we know it will cost us, but we don't realize that it will cost us more the longer we wait.

Too many of us face the darkness only when the pain of staying the same finally exceeds the pain of changing. For many, it's not an invitation but a demand we can no longer avoid that makes us deal with our monsters. When I was in college, my friend Josh's dad got fired from his preaching job. His dad continued to be a preacher; he just went to another church where he faithfully serves as their (very good) preacher.

Until then, I had never entertained the idea of getting fired. What I lacked in reality, I made up for in unfounded confidence. The thought that a church would think they are better off without me didn't even cross my mind. I even told Josh that if I ever got fired, there's no way I would continue to be a preacher.

I never ran toward the storm. I ran away by naively believing it couldn't happen to me.

I could have identified this as an opportunity for me to see the cancerous lies that had grown within my heart.

The lie that I am what I do.

The lie that my worth comes from what others say about me.

The lie that if I fail at work, I am a failure as a person.

Instead, I continued to run east until the storm finally caught up to me.

In the Darkness

I'VE BEEN IN CHURCH buildings all my life, yet on occasion I still get scared when I walk into a dark church building alone.

But I think I have an excuse.

I used to work at a church in which the light switches and the alarm were located on the opposite side from where I parked and entered the building. Many nights, with much haste and no drama, I traversed the dark lobby and exited the building in the sixty seconds between turning off the lights, turning on the alarm, and the alarm being activated.

But not this Wednesday night.

After seeing the last group of people in the lobby exit, I began my nightly routine. I walked through the building, turned the lights off and the alarm on, and briskly walked back under the nerve-racking sound of the alarm's beeping. As I came around a corner, I saw a glint of light bounce off a shiny white surface. I had never seen this shiny surface before, so I stepped closer to inspect the glimmering surface.

Then it moved.

It looked into my eyes.

And then it stood up, like Goliath over a shepherd boy.

Like David's smooth stone, my words slingshotted at the figure.

"Yo, Preacher Luke, it's me," said the disquieted giant, a six-foot, six-inch parishioner who had been homeless since his release from prison a few weeks before.

We both were upset at seeing each other.

He was upset because he had lost his place to sleep.

I was upset because if anyone had heard the words I said upon seeing him, I would have lost my job.

And that's why walking through a dark church building alone terrifies me, even though the same building doesn't create fear in me when people are present.

The person sitting with you when your child is in ICU can't cure your child, but somehow their presence makes it more bearable.

The person sharing a drink with you after you got fired can't get your job back, but their presence takes away some of the sting.

The family that adopts you for the first holiday after your spouse passes can't restore your family, but they can, ever so slightly, recharge your heart.

The darkness doesn't seem so dark when there is someone else with us. The darkness is demystified when someone hears our worst yet stays with us.

The Christian story gives us hope when we step into our darkness, because no matter how dark it appears, it's not too dark for God. Our faith is in a God who, in the person of Jesus, became a man, was crucified, was buried in a dark tomb, descended into darkness, and then three days later was resurrected. We shouldn't be afraid to go into the dark because God is not afraid to be in the darkness with us.

The last thing anyone wants when they face their monster is to be alone. And for us, the gospel is that we are never alone. We bravely go into the dark to face the monsters because we aren't alone. Over one hundred times in Scripture, God tells us not to be afraid, and often the next line is "for I am with you."

You have heard it said, "Here is the world. Beautiful and terrible things will happen. Don't be afraid."[9]

But I say unto you, "Here is your darkness. Beautiful and terrible things will happen. Don't be afraid to enter."

3

Destroy

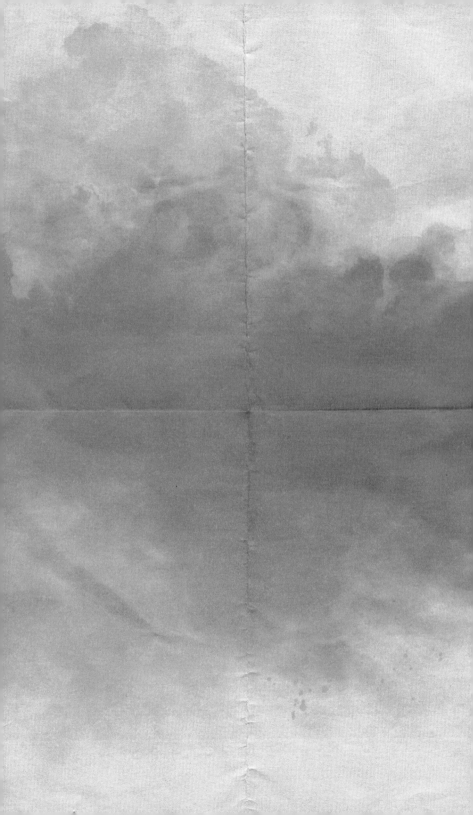

Werewolf

IN THE 1985 MOVIE *TEEN WOLF*, Michael J. Fox played a teenager who discovered that he was a werewolf. His monstrous secret didn't remain hidden for long, as the stress of a high school basketball game caused his werewolf-ness to appear and his secret to disappear. But Mr. J. Fox wasn't the first werewolf.

The word *werewolf* comes from the old English "man-wolf" or the Greek word for wolf-person, *lukanthropos*. *Anthro*, as in anthropology, meaning "person" and *Luke* from the Greek word for "a great sense of humor."

Some believe the first werewolf to have been the Greek king of Arcadia, Lycaon, who suffered this cruel fate at the hands of Zeus. In Zeus's defense, King Lycaon tried to test and mock the god's omniscience by serving Zeus the roasted flesh of Lycaon's own son. Yes, you read that correctly; Lycaon served Zeus the flesh of Lycaon's boy as a mockery to Zeus. Upon seeing King Lycaon's savage brutality, Zeus fittingly turned him into a savage beast, making the story of the werewolf King Lycaon a slightly darker werewolf story than Mr. J. Fox's version.

The typical werewolf appears as a normal man, but under the surface he's constantly resisting the urge to shape-shift into a wolf. In the right context with the right contact, his beastly powers appear. The Latin word for moon is *luna*, and contact with a full moon turns him into a beastly lunatic.

If all werewolves were just good point guards helping their high school basketball team end a three-year losing streak, then werewolves wouldn't have been included in the Middle Ages witch hunts. Sadly, the usual werewolf wasn't like Mr. J. Fox.

Beyond the surface fear of a werewolf hiding out in the woods and coming into your house to eat you is the subterranean and more substantial fear that the real monsters aren't out there hiding in the woods but are within you waiting to emerge.

The werewolf myth is grounded in the fear that, given the right context with the right contact, I am the one who can become the wrong person. The good that I want to do isn't what I do, but what I do is what I don't want to do.

In countless movies, we see the story line of a good guy who somehow does terrible things because terrible things have happened to him. In the 2009 movie *Law Abiding Citizen*, Gerard Butler plays a well-adjusted father until two men victimize and kill his wife and child in front of him. Upon seeing the justice system's toothless punishment of the criminals, Butler transforms from a law-abiding citizen—there's your movie title—into a monster who tortures and kills in the name of justice. Butler's grotesque actions would have been inconceivable for the well-adjusted father at the beginning of the story, but the right context shape-shifted him into a monster. This story has been told over and over again because we know that within us a force exists that is pulling and shaping us into the type of person that we shouldn't be.

In 1961, a twenty-eight-year-old Yale professor, Stanley Milgram, placed an ad in the *New Haven Register* asking for five hundred men to participate in an hour-long study of memory and learning for four dollars. Over the next two years, hundreds participated in the study, but the study they participated in wasn't the one they had signed up for. The American Psychological Association would pass guidelines in 1973 banning the type of deception used in this infamous study, which was officially published as the "Behavioral Study of Obedience" in 1963 in the *Journal of Abnormal Social Psychology*.

In Milgram's study, two men appeared to draw lots for the "teacher" or "learner" role, but it was rigged. The volunteer became the teacher every time while the second man, who was actually an actor, became the learner. The volunteer watched as the learner was strapped into a restraining chair with electrodes on his wrist. Then the volunteer went to an adjacent room to read a list of words to the learner, who was to memorize them and repeat them back. Each time the learner repeated the words incorrectly, the volunteer was to administer a shock. The shocks began at what the volunteer believed to be a "slight shock" of 15 volts and incrementally increased up to 450 volts, which was labeled "Danger: severe shock." As the actor in the learner role continued to give wrong answers, the response of the volunteer in the teacher role was shocking.

Despite hearing what the volunteer believed to be the cries of the learners (a recorded scream played over a speaker as no shocking actually took place), pounding on the wall, cries for mercy, and in some cases the ceasing of response as if the learner was unconscious, the volunteer persisted to administer shocks. Sixty-five percent of volunteers continued to shock the other person until the voltage reached the highest level of 450 volts. All volunteers continued shocking the learner until 300 volts.

Milgram intended to examine how obedient people would be, even at the expense of others. The experiments began a year after the trial of the Nazi soldier Adolf Eichmann in Jerusalem for war crimes, the trial during which Hannah Arendt coined the phrase "the banality of evil," describing how seemingly normal people could be obedient to the monstrous orders in the Holocaust. Following is a quote describing Eichmann's testimony of his almost "accidental" involvement in what might be the greatest atrocity in human history:

> You admitted that the crime committed against the Jewish people during the war was the greatest crime in recorded history, and you

admitted your role in it. But you said you had never acted from base motives, that you had never had any inclination to kill anybody, that you had never hated Jews, and still that you could not have acted otherwise and that you did not feel guilty. . . . You also said that your role in the Final Solution was an accident and that almost anybody could have taken your place, so that potentially almost all Germans are equally guilty.[1]

Building on the theory purported in the infamous Eichmann trial and the results of his study, Milgram claims that ordinary people under direction of authority figures can and will do monstrous things if they are in the right context with the right contact in the form of orders.

Years later, Arthur Miller, professor emeritus of psychology at Miami University, said of Milgram's participants:

They're not psychopaths, and they're not hostile, and they're not aggressive or deranged. They're just people, like you and me. If you put us in certain situations, we're more likely to be racist or sexist, or we may lie, or we may cheat. There are studies that show this, thousands and thousands of studies that document the many unsavory aspects of most people.[2]

A similar result to Milgram's study was found a decade later in the equally famous Stanford Prison Experiment. In the basement of Stanford's psychology building, which had been converted to look like a prison, volunteers pretended to be guards or inmates with such sadistic cruelty that the psychologists ended the planned two-week study on day six. The effect of the study, commonly known as the "Lucifer Effect," states that people's actions are more influenced by their context than by internal characteristics.

In the right context, with the right contact, we all can shape-shift into the wrong people. In a book about how monsters can save us, we shouldn't be so naive as to think that saving us is all our monsters can do to us. Monsters can destroy us, and anyone in a twelve-step program already knows this.

The Pull

I FOLLOWED A FRIEND and a dozen other guys into a cookie-cutter house next to a church. Seeing the "gently" used furniture's sparse placement and the overall non-home vibe, I assumed the church had purchased this house for meetings, such as the sex addicts anonymous meeting that my friend asked me to attend with him that evening.

After receiving a program, we carried metal folding chairs to the circle of what in a previous lifetime had been the house's living room. I tried to appear comfortable, but my viselike grip on the paper revealed my secret.

The meeting began with that night's leader mumbling through a reading of text in the program.

After his conclusion, men began to share their stories with the customary introduction, "Hi, I'm John, and I'm a sex addict."

Some shared victorious stories of sobriety and digging themselves out of the rubble their addictions had created. Others shared defeated stories of relapse and the emergence of freshly created rubble. The drive that when channeled properly leads to the life-giving warmth of intimacy in a covenanted relationship had become for this group a wildfire that burned down homes, careers, and their most important relationships.

Whichever side of the testimony they were on, sobriety or relapse, they all spoke with an awareness that something exists within them, a pull that makes them do what they don't want to do.

It's the same pull that the apostle Paul writes about in Romans 7:18–19:

> For I know that nothing good dwells within me, that is, in my flesh.
> I can will what is right, but I cannot do it. For I do not do the good
> I want, but the evil I do not want is what I do.

It's the same pull that causes the inspector of the 2012 Secret Service prostitution scandal to, years later, resign from the Department of Homeland Security after being implicated in his own incident with a prostitute.[3]

It's the pull that causes the singer of beautiful love songs to be outed for having multiple affairs on the love of their life.

It's the pull that causes politicians and pastors, who've devoted their lives to the betterment of society, to make destructive decisions that end in scandalous terminations.

Hypocrisy, contrary to popular opinion, is not just a religious problem; it's a human problem.

All people have the propensity to do and become what they don't ever want to be.

Yet far too often we disrespect this force.

It's seen in the language used when the politician after the scandal stands on a podium at a press conference to read a statement that says, "Mistakes have been made."

Mistakes?

Does the word *mistake* do this force justice? A mistake is when you make a wrong turn, call your girlfriend the wrong name, or go to the wrong restaurant.

It's not a mistake when you have to scheme for it to happen.

It's not a mistake when you know the damning ramification it will have on those you love, but you continue to do it for years.

Yet, we call it a mistake.

Maybe culture uses the anemic word *mistake* because church watered down the word that has been used for thousands of years to describe this force: sin.

When we in the church call what happens when you stub your toe and say the wrong colloquialism a sin, or when a person who doesn't go to a church service on Sunday is described as a sinner, the word *sin* loses its flavor like a tea bag that's been dipped in cup after cup after cup of hot water. We've spent the energy of the word *sin* flavoring uncouth words and suboptimal church attendance practices, so we've got nothing left to use to describe the life-destroying force that pulls us away from who we were intended to be.

Regardless of what you call it, a force exists within each of us that seeks to shape-shift us into what we and our Creator don't want us to become. For all the shallow reasons for not wanting to go into the darkness, there is a legitimate reason to avoid it—we might just see this force within us. We might experience the force that pulls us away from who we were created to be.

Cracks

MONSTERS CAN BE WARNING SIGNS that guide us into life and salvation, but let's not be so naive as to think that's the only direction they can pull us.

Leonard Cohen famously sang, "There is a crack, a crack in everything; that's how the light gets in."[4] I assume the passengers aboard the *Titanic* didn't share the Cohen-ish positivity toward cracks.

Cracks can let in life-giving grace and hope.

Cracks can also let in the water that drowns you in an iceberg-filled ocean.

I've seen money afford some people great opportunities to do good in the world. I've also seen others contorted into soul-shrunken joyless persons who believe that money makes them more important than others.

I've heard alcoholics say their addiction is a gift. I've also known of alcoholics who have drunk themselves to an isolated, lonely death.

I've heard people say getting fired was the best thing that ever happened to them. I've also seen others hold on to a crippling bitterness for decades after their termination.

Jesus accurately predicted that two of his disciples, Peter and Judas, would betray him during his time of greatest need. Soon after the prediction, Peter denied Jesus three times. Some scholars would even argue that Peter didn't just deny Jesus but cursed Jesus. Judas, after leaving everything he had to follow Jesus for years, turned on Jesus for the price the prophet Zechariah received years before for a single day's labor as a shepherd.

Peter and Judas both wronged Jesus, but Judas in his shame took his own life. Peter took his shame-filled life and gave it to Jesus. Then Jesus built his church upon Peter.

Monsters, like shame and failure, can be the light that guides you to salvation, but they can also be the force that collapses you into a form you weren't intended to be.

Curved

IN THE DOCUMENTARY *BLACKFISH*, filmmaker Gabriela Cowperthwaite details the sordid past of SeaWorld's treatment of orcas.

Most know the orca by their more popular moniker, killer whales, a name that orcas rarely live up to with humans in the wild. When housed at SeaWorld, however, orcas have become violent toward humans, killing at least one trainer. I'm no Jacques Cousteau, so I will leave it to marine biologists to determine the veracity of Cowperthwaite's claims of SeaWorld's mistreatment of orcas. But the effect of captivity upon the orca's appearance is a fitting metaphor for the subject at hand.

Cowperthwaite claims that SeaWorld's orcas, after being separated from their families, live in a prison-type environment that doesn't only alter their behavior but also affects their appearance, causing their dorsal fins to slump over. SeaWorld claims the orca's dorsal fin, which has no bone structure, collapses from gravity's pressure when an orca spends much time with their dorsal fin above the water's surface, whether at SeaWorld or in the wild.

Cowperthwaite doesn't agree. In the wild, 1 percent of male orcas' dorsal fins slump over, but at SeaWorld, all the males have flopped-over dorsal fins. "If they swim in one pattern, in circles, with no force of the ocean pushing against the dorsal fin in any way, it flops over. It's a part of their anatomy that marine biologists say you either 'use or lose,' and it's a useless tool in captivity."[5]

Instead of orcas' majestic dorsal fins towering above the water as in the wild, in captivity they bend over like the slumped shoulders of a downtrodden person or the tail between the legs of a cowering dog.

A force (whether that is gravity, as SeaWorld claims, or, as Cowperthwaite claims, inhumane treatment) has made orcas and their appearance less than they were intended to be.

Augustine described sin's function with the Latin phrase *incurvatus in se,* translated in English as "curved inward on itself." We were created in the image of God, standing tall like the dorsal fin of an orca, but sin collapses us into ourselves.

If the way of Jesus is an arms-wide-open posture, embracing all that the world and God have to offer, the way of sin is the opposite. It's a posture closed off to God and the world and only available to one's own darkness. A life controlled by this force collapses us into just a shell of our Creator's divine intention for us. This can happen to any of us in the right context with the right contact.

A divorced friend of mine was asked if he ever thought of getting married to his new girlfriend, and he said, "I wasn't meant to be married. I'm too selfish. I'll buy her a house right next to mine, but I'm not getting married again."

To be clear, there's nothing wrong with singleness. The Bible values singleness, as both Jesus and the apostle Paul were single. Paul even wished for the entire Corinthian church to remain single so as to live with undivided devotion to the Lord. Paul's singular devotion to the Lord is a far cry from my divorced friend's singular devotion to himself. God intends for none of us, whether single or married, to be so affected by selfishness that we can't share ourselves with others, but this happens when the dark force contorts us into less than our Creator's intent.

Shame can affect us in the same way.

The type of shame that grows out of bad decisions we have made by our own choosing can become a form of self-centeredness that elevates what we've done over what God has done for us. This type of shame centers our existence in what we've done (badly) when the gospel says the center of our identity is what God has done for all humanity in the person of Jesus. This type of shame feels honorable because it delineates right and wrong. But it actually dishonors God by devaluing what God has done to make us right. The self-centering force of this type of shame makes us focus only on ourselves.

This force, which presents in many forms ranging from addictions to self-righteousness, collapses us into ourselves, turning us into a shell of our Creator's intention for us. So we shouldn't have a Pollyanna attitude about monsters always being positive, especially considering that they don't affect only us.

Transform or Transmit

IN MARY SHELLEY'S NOVEL *FRANKENSTEIN*, Victor Frankenstein, a young scientist who is fascinated with creating life from nonliving matter, brings to life a hideous creature standing eight feet tall with yellow skin stretched so thin that it barely covers the monster's body. In horror of his own creation, Victor runs away from the monster. Rejected by his creator and unwelcomed by society, the monster's abandonment turns to anger at Victor Frankenstein. The monster enacts revenge by killing Victor's brother, Victor's best friend, and ultimately Victor's wife.

What do most of us call this monstrous creature?

Frankenstein.

I hate being the guy who corrects someone on a minor detail, like the person who returns from a week in Maui and now feels commissioned by Poseidon himself to make every person pronounce the word *Hawaii* correctly by inserting a hard stop between the two *i*'s.

But let me do that about this monster's name.

Despite commonly being known as Frankenstein, the monster's name isn't Frankenstein in Shelley's novel. Frankenstein is the name of the creator, not the creation. When we call the monster Frankenstein, we are subtly acting as if the monstrous behavior is about the creation while the creator, Victor, is simply the innocent victim.

When we call the monster by its longer but more accurate name, Frankenstein's monster, the possessive reminds us that the monster belongs to the creator. The pain inflicted on Victor's family was the result of Victor not wanting to deal with what he had created.

As Richard Rohr says, "If you don't transform your pain, then you will transmit your pain."[6]

Victor Frankenstein created a monster but couldn't deal with the hideous pain; so instead of transforming it, he transmitted the pain to the ones he loved the most.

Achan

THERE'S A STORY about the Israelites in which God promises that if they march around the town of Jericho for seven days, the walls of Jericho will fall and the city will become theirs. On day seven when the walls fall, God specifically instructs the Israelites to bring the silver, gold, bronze, and iron to the treasury of the Lord, but everything else is devoted to destruction. And to ensure the Monster of More doesn't convince anyone to take the items devoted to destruction, God says not to even go near them.

The Israelites march around Jericho for seven days, an exhausting experience that it feels as if my wife ensures I re-create every time she brings me to Target. Then, on day seven, the walls collapse. All of Israel obeys the command to take to God what is God's and leave to destruction what is devoted to it.

Except one man,

Achan,

who took some devoted items.

Israel continued its conquest, stumbling into the town of Ai, a town as small as its name. The Israelite spies felt the small town required only a small delegation of three thousand Israelites. To everyone's surprise, the tiny army of Ai overpowered them.

The Israelite leader, Joshua, cries out to God, feeling that God wronged Israel by leading them across the Jordan River only to have them lose this battle. God responds:

> Israel has sinned; they have transgressed my covenant that I imposed on them. They have taken some of the devoted things; they have stolen, they have acted deceitfully, and they have put them among their own belongings. Therefore the Israelites are unable to stand before their enemies; they turn their backs to their enemies, because they have become a thing devoted for destruction themselves. I will be with you no more, unless you destroy the devoted things from among you. (Josh. 7:11–12)

Look at the pronouns used.

"*They* have taken."

"*They* have stolen."

"*They* have acted deceitfully."

How many stole?

One man.

Achan.

But everyone felt the pain because Achan couldn't transform the pull the Monster of More had on him. Monsters are personal, but their consequences are rarely only personal. When we don't transform our pain, we transmit it to those around us.

Talk

HE COULDN'T FATHOM why the words he never wanted to say were not only being said, but also being said to the people he least wanted to say them to. When coworkers did the most inconsiderate of things, he didn't respond with such language. When a restaurant got his order wrong, he was patient. When someone did the one-finger wave in traffic, he laughed it off. The vitriolic words flowed out of his mouth only when talking to the people he most loved. He couldn't make sense of it, so he turned to his pastor for help.

"Did your dad talk to your mom this way?" I asked.

"No," he responded.

"Did your mom talk to your dad this way?"

"No."

"Did either of your parents talk to you this way?"

"No."

I was dumbfounded until he let this line slip out of his mouth:

"The only time I ever hear those words is when I do something stupid."

"Who says those words to you when you do something stupid?" I asked.

"Me," he replied.

"What do you mean 'me'?"

"I talk to myself that way. Ever since I was a kid, I've talked like this to myself when I do something stupid."

The "you idiot's" and the "what's wrong with you's" and their more premium-cable versions created the refrain in his own head when he made mistakes. But that negativity didn't stay within his own head. He eventually transmitted that vitriol to the people he loved the most.

Self-talk easily becomes spouse-talk, child-talk, and friend-talk if it's not transformed.

The self-talk could have been a warning sign to him that a negative force existed within him and an invitation to intentionally choose to listen to the voice that speaks truth and love. But instead, that force had free reign over his heart, pulling him away from life and love.

Generational

As Ms. Nolan finished picking up her classroom at the end of the day, she noticed that her desk drawer was missing three items: an envelope with thirty-eight dollars, a pack of gum, and a plastic flower. After double-checking to ensure she hadn't misplaced those three items elsewhere in the classroom or out in her car, she concluded that they had been stolen by one of her first-grade students.

The next morning, she asked her class if anyone had taken any items from her desk with the promise that if the student returned the stolen items now, there would be no punishment. With no takers of the amnesty offer, the teacher told the class she would begin checking backpacks.

As she worked her way through the first row of students, a hand was raised in the back row. The teacher stopped her backpack search and made her way to the hand's owner. His chin quivered. An alligator tear trickled down his cheek as he confessed to taking three items—an envelope with thirty-eight dollars, a pack of gum, and a plastic flower—despite the teacher not telling the class what had been stolen. The items were at the boy's home, but he promised to return them the next day.

At pickup that afternoon, the teacher informed the mother of her son's deed, his confession, and his willingness to return the items, while also informing the mother that because of her son's honesty he wasn't going to face any consequences.

"My son didn't steal your stuff," the mother snapped.

"What?" Ms. Nolan said in shock.

"He didn't steal nothing."

"Your son confessed to it. Even saying the exact dollar figure," Ms. Nolan responded.

"I didn't see that stuff. He didn't steal it," the mother said.

Seeing his mother's response, the boy joined in. "Yeah, I didn't steal it."

The mother continued, "He only said that because he was scared."

The boy's chin, emboldened by his mother's support, turned defiant.

The mother's inability to deal with the shame of having a son who stole something from his first-grade teacher caused her to transmit her pain onto her son, not only making him lie in that moment but also enabling more destructive behavior in his future.

This is the heart of generational sin today. Not that God punishes children for their parents' sins but that the effects of sin are transmitted from generation to generation by parents who don't transform their pain.

The Contest

JOHN STEINBECK IN *EAST OF EDEN* SAYS, "We all have one story, and it is the same story; the contest of good and evil within us."[7]

Naiveté to the pull of evil within us leaves us oblivious to the person we could become.

The Canadian psychologist Jordan Peterson developed a plan called Self Authoring in which participants develop two scenarios for the next five years of their life: a best-case scenario and a worst-case scenario.

As a pastor, I see these scenarios played out in real time in front of me.

On the one hand, I see this when I go to a bereaved family's home to prepare a eulogy about their deceased loved one. I hear adult children, grandkids, sons-in-law, siblings, and a spouse pour out effusive praise. I've seen this with widows, who glowingly describe the half a century they spent with the love of their lives. And I see the joyfully content lives created by one five-year best-case scenario after another.

On the other hand, I've also helped pack up the moving truck for a spouse who left her husband after his addiction had overcome him and the pain had been transmitted to those he loved the most. I've fought back tears while children describe how their mother's selfishness made them never want to see her again.

If we don't know that we are in a contest that can lead us down either of these paths, we are destined to lose the contest.

So let me ask you, in five years, whom would the power of your fears, anxieties, obsessions, and insecurities turn you into?

Would you curve in so much that you lose the ability to receive love?

Would the darkness turn the lights out in your home?

Would your guilt and shame become the center of your identity?

This dark force does exist. Don't be naive to its power or oblivious to its presence.

The force trying to fold you in on yourself exists, but it doesn't have to win. It doesn't have to destroy you; it can also deliver you.

4

Deliver

Swallowed

IN THE FEW SECONDS he'd been in the water, his brain miraculously had the cognitive functioning to cycle through each of the worst-case scenarios one could imagine while being alone in the middle of the sea. Just a few days before, when he'd rushed out the door to embark on this spur-of-the-moment journey across the globe, his wife had asked why the hurry. His brain sluggishly vacillated from one bad excuse to the next. His excuses were so bad that he didn't even blame his wife for disbelieving every word he said. But now, his brain wasn't sluggish. On hyperspeed, his brain brought forth one terrible option after the next. One moment, his brain recalled accounts of fishermen describing beasts larger than boats. The next moment, he replayed the legends from his youth of little boys wading into the water, never to return.

Earlier that morning, when he had paid his way onto the boat, the seas were tranquil and the skies clear. Now the seas were untenable when within a boat, not that he was anymore. In the water, with nothing to defend himself from the wind and waves, he knew he'd soon experience one of his ominously imagined scenarios.

He gasped for breath out of panic, but it never came.

He had been yanked below.

He was pulled deeper and deeper and then suddenly . . . released.

Orienting himself, he looked for the stormy surface and, to his surprise, he found it. The darkness had turned into daylight. The angry sea had calmed. Stunned by the split-second change in weather, he forgot to swim up.

But then he felt the pull of a vacuum in the water, and it all went dark around him.

"This is what I get for running away from God," Jonah thought as the beast swallowed him whole.

Monster Levels

MONSTERS EXIST FOR THE SINGULAR PURPOSE of destruction—whether that monster be a zombie, a mother-in-law, or, worse yet, your mother-in-law reincarnate as a zombie—but they present on different levels.

We can see these two different levels in the story of Jonah. God directs the Jewish prophet Jonah to go to Nineveh, the capital city of Israel's violent oppressor, Assyria. Jonah, like any Jewish person, doesn't want to be anywhere near Assyria. Jonah puts his rebellious feelings into action, going the opposite direction of God's command by way of a boat. A storm threatens the ship. The unbelieving sailors throw the prophet in the water, hoping to appease his God. Upon entering the water, the first level of monster appears.

Level-one monsters are the physically terrifying kind like the Philistine giant Goliath or Frankenstein's monster. The mere sight of their stature or the sound of their voice makes you want to run like the Israelites did from Goliath. For Jonah, it's the man-eating fish. But this level of monster, for all its fear-inducing scales, teeth, and claws, still lacks in one thing.

Steven Pressfield describes what I'm referring to as level-one monsters in a piece about writing villains. When he writes *villains*, think monsters:

> The easiest villain to write is the external villain. The Alien. The shark in *Jaws*. The Terminator. Doc Ock, Bane, Immortan Joe. . . .

External villains present existential threats to our physical existence. These . . . will kill you, eat you, freeze you, boil you.

The problem with external villains, though they may occasionally deliver bestseller sales and boffo box office, is they don't often bring out the best in the stars who must confront them.

Why? Because the stars only have to duel these villains on one level (and the most superficial level, at that): the physical.[1]

These monsters are like the popcorn we eat while watching them. It's fine for what it is, but it will never fill you up, because level-one monsters can't bring out what's buried within your heart. They will make you run, they will make you hide, but they can't make you grow.

When we make the story of Jonah only about the fish that consumes him, we stay on the superficial level. It's then just a children's story, which never lets the story challenge what's within Jonah's heart or our own hearts.

Deeper Level

THE MOST MONSTROUS FORCE in the story of Jonah wasn't the fish that swallowed Jonah's body, but the monster that had swallowed Jonah's heart.

After three nights in the stomach of the whale, Jonah is spit up on the shore because,

you know,

you can't keep a good man down. Jonah goes to preach to Nineveh. Nineveh repents; everyone, even the animals, puts on sackcloth and ashes, a not-so-subtle reminder of the story's humor. But Jonah is angry about their repentance:

But this was very displeasing to Jonah, and he became angry. He prayed to the LORD and said, "O LORD! Is not this what I said while I was still in my own country? That is why I fled to Tarshish at the beginning; for I knew that you are a gracious God and merciful, slow to anger, and abounding in steadfast love, and ready to relent from punishing." (Jon. 4:1–2)

The real monster in this story isn't the fish that consumed his body but the hatred that consumed Jonah's heart. Jonah didn't run away from Nineveh because he was afraid of the bodily harm the Ninevites would exact on him. He was afraid of the boundless love of God that would be extended to the people Jonah hated.

As the wisdom of the western movie genre teaches us, if you are out for revenge, you'd better dig two graves: one for them and one for you. Even after three days in the belly of the fish, when Jonah was spit out on dry land, he wasn't resurrected a new man because hatred still consumed him.

The deeper level of monsters invites us into our own hearts. Level-two monsters prove that the line of good and evil is never between us and them but right down the middle of me.

It's the harder monster to face because it will not be stopped with a gun. It's also the more rewarding monster because it offers us a chance to grow.

Steven Pressfield says this phenomenon plays out in the movie *Silver Linings Playbook*:

> The villain in *Silver Linings Playbook* is interior. It exists inside Bradley Cooper's head. The villain is his obsession, fueled by his bipolar disorder, with winning back his wife Nikki, whom he has alienated by his extravagant behavior in the past. . . .
>
> What a hero Bradley will be if he can somehow, either alone or aided by Jennifer [Lawrence], see the real love that's staring him in

the face and recognize this Nikki-self-delusion for the monster it is—and *change himself.*

Spoiler alert: he does. . . .

That's a star. . . .

What made that star was the scale and depth of the villain he (and she) had to fight.[2]

What made Jennifer Lawrence and Bradley Cooper stars wasn't the kind of monster that resides in a cave but the type of monster that resides in the heart. It's the same kind of monster that Jonah refused to face. And it's the same kind of monster that you are going to have to befriend. Your monster probably isn't going to make you a movie star, but it can make you a saint. As Thomas Merton taught, to be a saint is to be our truest self. Your monster can help you become your truest self by forcing you to engage with the internal issues we'd all rather, like Jonah, ignore in our own hearts.

Jesus implores us to make the same move toward inner work: "You have heard that it was said . . . , 'You shall not murder.' . . . But I say to you that if you are angry with a brother or sister, you will be liable to judgment" (Matt. 5:21–22).

The behavior modification of the teaching of Moses, which Jesus references, is a helpful start, but Jesus pushes deeper, past mere external actions. Abstaining from committing murder doesn't require you to go deeper to engage the animus in your heart that caused you to want to murder. Just as getting rid of the fish that swallowed Jonah wouldn't expose the true monster of hatred that had consumed Jonah's heart.

Monsters can be the cracks that let the light in because they get you to access the location where you most need salvation. When you go into the dark, you feel the destructive pull, but you can also feel the invitation to inspect what resides within your heart.

The Invitation

A WISE MAN AND A FOOLISH MAN are in a forest on a stormy night. The way you tell them apart is by what they do when the lightning strikes. The foolish man looks up to see the lightning race across the darkened sky. The wise man takes the brief moment of illumination from the lightning to see which path he is on and where he needs to go.

The foolish man stares at the lightning, part scared stiff by the sound of the accompanying thunder and part in awe of the brightness of the sky.

The wise man overcomes his fear of what the lightning could do to him and instead uses the lightning's evanescent illumination to get his bearings about both his current location and his path home.

For us to avoid the way of the fool, we must allow the moments when monsters illuminate our paths to be valued invitations to assess who we are and where we are headed. When I feel the Monster of More saying that I don't have enough, I must be wise enough to see that as an invitation to inspect the lies that reside within my own heart. When the Monster of Comparison makes me size up my own existence to someone else, I must be mature enough to see that as an invitation to investigate what's lacking in my heart to cause me to find my identity in how I stack up to someone else. These invitations exist to access life, but many refuse to be delivered. In doing so, they unknowingly choose the way of destruction.

For Jonah, the invitation wasn't one that he liked. The terms went like this:

Jonah, your heart is full of hatred. God's heart is full of love. Jonah, you despise the Ninevites. God loves the Ninevites. The invitation is to let your hate-filled heart become transformed into a love-filled heart like God's heart.

For some of us, the invitation is just as unwelcome. The lightning reveals offensive terms because the life you've received isn't the life you want. Your career, home life, health, social standing, income, or whatever other facet of life isn't how you imagined it to be. These undesired terms create pain. You either run from this pain, thereby transmitting it to the people all around you, which is similar to what Jonah did by running from God and dragging the sailors into an ill-fated voyage. Or you transform your heart by accepting God's invitation and receiving what God has for you.

Not everyone accepts the invitation given to them.

Jonah didn't accept the invitation. To be exact, Jonah refused the invitation three times, saying he would rather die than live in a world in which God loves the people Jonah hates.

> And now, O LORD, please take my life from me, for it is better for me to die than to live. (Jon. 4:3)

> He said, "It is better for me to die than to live." (4:8)

> But God said to Jonah, "Is it right for you to be angry about the bush?" And he said, "Yes, angry enough to die." (4:9)

Jonah's not the only one. Many of us choose to hold on to cancerous lies that pull us away from life rather than accept the invitation to the reality in front of us. Many of us would rather hold on to our idealized picture of what we deserve, no matter the cost, instead of receiving the gift of a perfectly imperfect life.

More Room

YEARS AGO, I achieved the special milestone that solidifies a preacher as a real preacher: I was called a false teacher.

It's the preacher-equivalent of a child losing their first tooth.

I sought guidance from a friend who's been called a false teacher his fair share of times. His email response,

They've

given

you

a

gift.

I wouldn't have initially considered someone questioning my character, integrity, and truthfulness to be a gift, but now I see his wisdom.

As is the case with many of the most substantial gifts we receive, we should be grateful they don't come with a receipt because we would have immediately returned them. But with the right mixture of patience and time, we can become grateful, because in all things God is working for the good.

In his book *What Good Is God?* Philip Yancey gave the following perplexing title to an essay: "Why I Wish I Was an Alcoholic." But that title wasn't perplexing to a few of my friends.

My friend Chris, who has a PhD in nuclear physics from Duke, left the faith that he learned as a child in a Southern Baptist church over intellectual issues reconciling faith and science. What brought him back to faith was a need to make sense of his brokenness, which was only revealed to him by his alcoholism.

Another friend, James, despite losing almost everything—job, money, and worst of all, his wife—because of his alcoholism, doesn't regret the past. Instead, he's grateful for what his alcoholism has taught him.

Both of their stories express what Yancey says in his essay. The following is an excerpt in which Yancey tells what one of his alcoholic friends said:

> I prayed every day that God would take away my thirst for drink, and every day when I woke up my first thought was Jack Daniel's whiskey. Then one day I realized my craving for drink was the very reason I pray every day. My weakness drives me to God.[3]

I'm most certain that Yancey doesn't truly wish to have alcoholism, but I think he's aware of the gift that even addiction can be to you because of where it can point you. Or more specifically, to whom it can point you.

Addictions point many to isolation, poverty, and jail, but they can also be the gift that reveals the need to pray. The English mystic Julian of Norwich says that sin is behovely* "because it brings us to self-knowledge, knowledge of our own fallibility, which in turn moves us to seek God."[4]

Eugene Peterson paraphrases the verse of the Beatitudes commonly translated "Blessed are the poor in spirit, for theirs is the kingdom of heaven" in this way: "You're blessed when you're at the end of your rope. With less of you there is more of God and his rule" (Matt. 5:3 Message).

Which could be paraphrased for some of us this way:

You're blessed when you feel out of control, unable to keep your world spinning and your life in order, because then you realize that you never were the one in control to begin with.

You're blessed when you feel empty and desperate, because then you finally know the One who fills you.

---

*That is, advantageous or necessary.

You're blessed when you feel like giving up, because then you are able to give your life over to the One who can sustain you.

You're blessed when you don't have what you think you need, because then you are aware of what is truly a necessity.

You're blessed when you crave a drink, because then you can be aware of the One whose cup will satiate you.

You're blessed when people critique you unfairly, because then you can start to listen to the voice that speaks the truth about you.

You're blessed when hatred fills your heart, because only then do you realize how empty you truly are.

Point or Prop

THE POINT OF JONAH'S STORY wasn't that he was consumed by a fish but that he was consumed by hatred. The monstrous fish was a prop; the point was the hatred within his heart. The fish functioned as God's means of getting Jonah to investigate Jonah's heart to see the monster within himself.

Many of us have been consumed, hopefully not by a fish or for that matter any of the following creatures: anaconda, bear (black, brown, or grizzly), or a pack of ants or buzzards. But we have been consumed by the lies that we are what others say about us, we are what we have, and we are what we do. The gift that God gives us is to let these monstrous props direct us to the real point.

Some believe God orchestrates every adverse circumstance in life to teach us a lesson. I don't, but I have seen how God uses adversity, like my job loss, as a prop to force me to engage with what's in my heart. And God can do the same in your life. God can use your monsters to be the warning—the prop—you need to transform you into being who God created you to be.

AN INTERLUDE
An Open Letter to Dwayne Johnson

Dear Mr. The Rock,

I've always loved you, DJ. I think we could be friends, maybe even best friends.

There's only one time I ever did something less than supportive of the Rock.

I once was the speaker at a Baptist youth camp while in grad school. I think they, the Baptists, call that position "camp pastor." I'm from the churches of Christ, so that sounds weird to me. But anyway, one of the youths there, a strapping young fella who started as middle linebacker on his high school football team, was called "the Rock" by his friends because he looked like a smaller version of you. Long story short, I ended up getting in a friendly wrestling match with him. One thing led to another, and I might have broken the Little Rock's arm.

Coincidentally, I haven't been invited back as camp pastor again.

But that's the closest thing I've ever come to wronging the name of the real Dwayne Johnson.

I've supported your work for as long as I can remember. I watched your first movie and almost every one since then. I've seen you defeat mummies, earthquakes, gravity by flying a Ford out of a plane, the CIA (while carrying Kevin Hart), a video game that came to life (also while carrying Kevin Hart), a burning skyscraper, and a gigantically mutated gorilla, wolf, and alligator at the same time. But one thing I miss seeing you tackle in a movie is something that a gun, a truck, a helicopter, or money can't defeat.

I'm sure stepping away from being an action hero will cost you, but I think you've got more to offer than just fighting scary monsters on the outside. I think you should do a movie in which you overcome a bigger monster, like a monster that lives inside of you.

Yours truly,
Luke

P.S. Hit me up when you are ready to do a podcast.

The Three Universal Monsters

MONSTER-OLOGISTS* point to major monster types that transcend continents, cultures, and centuries, such as water monsters. The Cherokee people, a Native American tribe from the southeastern United States, feared the Uktena, a man-eating aquatic serpent monster that looked like a rattlesnake with horns. Other Native American cultures have similar fear-inducing horned water monsters—for example, the Iroquois tribe's Onyare or the Algonquin tribe's W'akuk. And across the big pond is the Kraken, another aquatic monster minus the horns but with giant squid features that terrorized Europe.

Which begs the question, Why do similar monsters appear across continents, cultures, and centuries?

---

*Technically not a real title, but it should be.

Option one: a singular transcontinental aquatic monster exists whose Phelps-ian swimming acumen should curtail all non-pool swimming.

Option two: these similar monsters across continents and cultures point to humanity's universal fears. Because no matter how divergent our land, language, or lore, inside our hearts we aren't that different.

My experience as a pastor makes me choose option two. I see the same struggles with expressions as unique as the different names for water monsters. Underneath the varied fur, flesh, and fangs, they are the same struggles repeated over and over again. As Solomon said, there's nothing new under the sun. Our monsters are unique in their expression because they've been influenced and affected by our particularities, yet they are common to all. They are both unique to us and universal to everyone.

The great Catholic scholar and priest Henri Nouwen said we all are tempted to believe three lies:[1]

I am what other people say or think about me.

I am what I have.

I am what I do.

In the next section of this book, these three lies will become the three universal monsters of comparison, more, and success. While presented uniquely in each individual person, these three monsters traverse continents, cultures, and centuries to haunt all of us.

Using the story of Jonah as an archetype for how to befriend our monsters, we will look at these monsters through the following four questions:

1. What's the prop?

2. What's the pull?

3. What's the point?

4. How does the light get in?

For reference, here's a way to interpret these questions through Jonah:

1. The prop was the fish that swallowed him. It appeared to be the centerpiece of the story, but in hindsight it was only a level-one monster that got the hero moving.

2. The pull was Jonah's hatred for the Ninevites that conformed him to a closed-off posture that couldn't receive (but could run from) God's intentions for his life.

3. The point of the story was not the fish that swallowed Jonah but the monster of hatred that consumed Jonah's heart.

4. The light could have come in by the transforming of Jonah's hateful heart to see the value in his enemies and God's boundless love. Sadly for Jonah, this didn't happen.

Warning: As we engage with these monsters, don't be naive. These monsters can pull us away from life as they contort us into a shell of God's intention for us. But they can also be the invitation to access the deeper part of our souls and to become our truest selves if we learn to befriend them.

As my friend Annie F. says, the person I want to be is usually on the other side of where I would have given up.

When it gets hard, don't run.

When it gets disorienting, don't let go.

When it gets painful, don't give up.

Let's go into the darkness, so we can experience the light.

5

Comparison

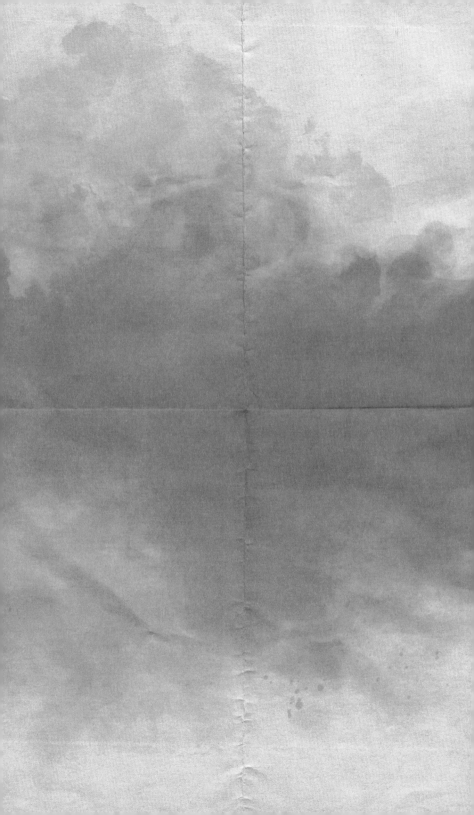

5.1 THE PROP

More Than Me

BIG SMALLS

AT THE BEGINNING of my sophomore year in college, my first year in Texas after transferring from a school in Arkansas, my friend Geoff invited me to attend Grace's Bible study. The Bible study had a weird name, but so did my friend Geoff. So I went.

I expected a dozen people studying the Bible. You know, the basic mixture of the words *Bible* and *study*. But everything is bigger in Texas, even the Bible studies. Instead of a few people holding highlighters and their NIV Study Bible, I saw a full band, large stacks of speakers, bright lights, and over a thousand students in attendance.

I looked for Grace, the Bible study's magnanimous host, with no success. Upon further inspection, the event's name was actually Grace Bible Study. The *s* was left out, just like my beloved a cappella singing.

My Christian tradition, the churches of Christ, at that point in time used only voices for music (aka a cappella). Once as a high school student, I had wandered like the prodigal son from my flock to attend a worship service with a band. My high school friend Justin had invited me to his Pentecostal church for what was referred to as a "worship service."

But to me it seemed more like a séance.

People hopped around in the dark to the blaring music sung by someone on a darkened stage who I'm still not certain wasn't Ozzy

Osbourne. Halfway through the event, I was running out of the build-ing like someone fleeing an overly friendly prom date.

Upon seeing Grace Bible Study's band onstage, I made a mental note of the location of the exits. I'd suffer through instrumental praise music as long as there wasn't any snake handling, flag waving, or people raising their hands over their head. I would accept a hand raised to shoulder height (aka a gentleman's hand-raising), but no farther.

The band was loud, yet with each song my fear diminished that an animal would be sacrificed onstage. Thirty minutes later, the music stopped. I felt like you do at an amusement park when the roller coaster makes that jarring stop in the station at the conclusion of your ride. Your heart is still beating over 150 beats per minute, but you no longer think at any second you could die.

As the band left the stage, an overly tall man in his midtwenties stepped onstage.

"Hi, my name is Matt. Turn in your Bibles to Romans."

Maybe it was Acts, Galatians, or another book of the Bible. Which-ever one it was, it didn't register. I was too stunned that someone not from the churches of Christ would actually preach from the Bible. I assumed Baptists only preached from *The Purpose Driven Life*.

Arrogance and ignorance make for happy dance partners, or at least they did for me. Matt's preaching quickly overcame my judgmental heart. No preacher had ever connected with me like Matt. When he stopped talking, I was genuinely disappointed. From that week on, I'd skip intramurals and rearrange my class schedules to attend.

Most baby preachers spend their first few years preaching in someone else's voice because they haven't yet found their own voice. I wanted to be honest, challenging, raw, and engaging, so as an eighteen-year-old just starting to preach, I parroted Matt's voice. Matt was a Calvinist, because no one is perfect, so I read the people he quoted in his sermons, such as Jonathan Edwards and John Piper. It was the theological equivalent of the old question, Would you jump off a cliff if all of your friends were predestined to?

Three years later, Matt announced that he was leaving to pastor a small Baptist church in the Dallas suburb of Highland Village and I was asked to replace Matt as the new speaker at Grace Bible Study.

I was beyond excited to serve in a ministry that had a substantial impact on moving me away from my sectarian attitudes about my denomination and worship. I was honored that I could now have the chance to play a role in the formation of other students. I took the job beause I believed in what the ministry could do, but I also wanted to be like Matt.

As a twenty-one-year-old, I assumed that I would slide in as the new speaker and have the same success as Matt. I assumed that my preaching would be transformative and that speaking requests would flood my email just like they did for Matt. I expected to be just like Matt, because I had no clue how much of an outlier Matt turned out to be.

I didn't know that Matt's small church of a couple hundred in the suburbs of Dallas would grow after his arrival into The Village, a church of over ten thousand people. I didn't know that his sermon podcast would regularly be one of the highest ranked on iTunes. I didn't know that Matt Chandler would become one of the biggest names in American Christianity. I didn't know that almost two decades later I would still consider him to be one of the two best communicators I had ever been around.

If so, I never would have started comparing myself to him.

But I did.

I never intentionally designated Matt as the standard for what I wanted my career to look like, but I needed something to make sense of how I was doing. I subconsciously decided that he would be the standard, but that didn't work out too well.

The following story sums up how well that comparison game went for me.

At the first Bible study of my second semester of preaching, we had a special reunion service celebrating Grace's ten-year anniversary. The previous speakers, Matt and his predecessor, returned that Tuesday night so all three of us could preach, kind of like the ghosts of Grace past, present, and future.

The following week, we were back to a normal Bible study where I alone would preach. At the beginning of the service, I stood in the back of the sanctuary while wearing a wireless microphone over my ear (a clear giveaway that I would be talking onstage). A college student walked up to me and asked, "Is Matt preaching tonight?"

I said, "No, I'm sorry, that was last week, but this week—"

Before I finished my sentence, she had turned around and was walking out the glass door.

Like the reflex that makes us stare at the wreckage after a car accident, I couldn't stop watching this student walk away because I wasn't the person she wanted to hear. With each step across the parking lot, her figure appeared smaller and smaller, which is exactly what the Monster of Comparison was doing to my self-image while preaching in Matt's shadow. Every time someone expressed how much they missed Matt, every mention of the good old days at Grace, every "remember when Matt said," my self-esteem took one step further away.

I never would have imagined that getting to speak at the biggest Bible study I had ever seen could make me feel small.

But it did.

COMPARE

MOST OF US don't intentionally set out to compare ourselves to others.

Like someone falling off a ladder, we reach out to grab whatever is around us, no matter how precarious, because it's disorienting trying to understand how your life is going. We don't have a rule book that determines what your family life should be like, how much money you should have, or how far along your career should have advanced, but we do have people all around us who can easily become the standard by which we measure ourselves.

Early on, the comparison is to which kids on the playground are the fastest runners or who has the most classmates coming to their birthday party. Even with age, we rarely outgrow making comparisons, despite the cost.

For example, let me give you two options for your compensation package in your next job.

Option one: you earn 90K and your coworkers earn 70K.

Option two: you earn 100K and your coworkers earn 150K.

Which compensation package would you choose?

Did you choose option one? If so, you are like most people.

Research shows people would choose to live with less total money as long as it is more, in comparison, than the people around them. Research also shows that we'd do the same thing in regard to vacation time. We would choose the option of two weeks of vacation when our coworkers get one week, instead of the option of four weeks of vacation when our coworkers get six weeks.[1]

Dizzying fear will make us reach for almost anything and compare almost everything.

Adam Alter, in his book *Irresistible* on the rise of addictive technology, writes about the reason Facebook's founder Mark Zuckerberg acquired Instagram from its cofounder Kevin Systrom: "It's easy to see why Zuckerberg chose to acquire Instagram. He and Systrom shared a similar insight: that people are endlessly driven to compare themselves to others."[2]

Alter goes on to observe that the primary reason we now take photos is to share those memories with others. Back in the 1980s, we did this by making our friends (or grandchildren) sit through slideshows of our recent vacation or trip to the Holy Land, but today we compare our experiences in real time.

This monster says I am what others think or say about me based on how I compare to them. But despite what our eyes tell us, the people I compare myself to aren't the point. They are just a prop, inviting me to go deeper, if I can resist its pull.

5.2 THE PULL

Identity Crisis

SLIDING SCALE

He stood head and shoulders over everyone as the paragon of a military man turned politician, but his good looks and résumé didn't matter when the new guy appeared. Not only was the new guy one of his high-ranking soldiers, but he was also his son's best friend. The laurels on which he should have been resting should have allowed him to celebrate the next man up, but when the people began singing of the new guy's successes, his self-esteem couldn't survive:

> Saul has slain his thousands,
>   and David his tens of thousands. (1 Sam. 18:7 NIV)

For Jesus's followers who've been formed by his teachings on turning the other cheek and loving your enemies, it might be hard to hear the song of King Saul's and David's military exploits, but we can still easily acknowledge that a thousand people is a lot of dead people.

Let's put this in context with the American sniper Chris Kyle, the US Navy SEAL veteran who served four tours in Iraq and has been credited with the most kills of any sniper in American history with 160.

Saul was credited with thousands.

Saul should have been enjoying a final victory lap before riding off into the sunset. Instead, David's arrival and success infuriated Saul because Saul no longer sat at the top of the scale.

The pull of comparison is to place our value on a sliding scale, which results in an identity crisis.

When we look up to the person with ten thousand, we slide down into insecurity. When we look down at the person with only 160, we slide up into arrogance.

Insecurity and arrogance appear to be polar opposites, but they are both equal expressions of the identity crisis created by comparison. The opposite of arrogance isn't insecurity, just as the opposite of insecurity isn't arrogance. The opposite of both is contentment.

Fr. Ronald Rolheiser says it this way:

> So much of our unhappiness comes from comparing our lives, our friendships, our loves, our commitments, our duties, our bodies and our sexuality to some idealized and non-Christian vision of things which falsely assures us that there is a heaven on earth. When that happens, and it does, our tensions begin to drive us mad, in this case to a cancerous restlessness.[3]

Comparing ourselves to others produces inferiority and insecurity because we are attempting to steady ourselves on an object that can never balance us, creating "a cancerous restlessness."

FORGOTTEN

AFTER THE SERVICE ENDED in which I was a guest preacher at a church in the small West Texas town of Hamby, a familiar voice barked in my direction from a few pews behind me.

"It's a good thing you are a better preacher than you were a pole-vaulter."

Before I even turned around, I knew that perplexing statement had originated from the legendary track coach Don Hood, my pole-vaulting coach from my time as a walk-on for Abilene Christian University's track team.

I've tried to decipher that comment for years. On the one hand, words like *good* and *better* imply positivity. On the other hand, back in my time under his tutelage, Coach Hood frequently expressed dissatisfaction with my pedestrian foot speed with colloquialisms such as "Luke's problem is the grass keeps growing under his feet while he's running."

How does one compare the quality of one's preaching to one's poor performance in pole-vaulting? One activity involves a lot of physical exertion and sweating, and when executed poorly it can leave one with brain damage. The other activity is pole-vaulting.

A comparison of preaching to pole-vaulting or you to someone else in your field or a sibling always leads to confusion, because when we compare ourselves to others we forget who we are.

We remember our appearance.

We remember our bank account.

We remember our social standing.

We remember our wins and our losses.

But we don't remember what truly matters.

We don't remember that our meaning doesn't sit on a sliding scale.

We don't remember that our identity isn't tied to what others say about us.

We don't remember the deep abiding love that we've been given by our heavenly parent.

AMERICAN IDOL

THINK OF THE WORD often used to describe a person we greatly admire or want to be like. We say that person is our idol.

Idol, as in the thing the Bible always says is bad.

While the Israelites waited in the wilderness for Moses to return from Mount Sinai with the stone tablets, the Israelites became scared that they were alone. So they asked Moses's brother, Aaron, to build them an idol. They couldn't stand the uneasy discomfort of being alone, so they reached for balance in an idol. Just like we do today.

Scripture dislikes the idols of old because they replaced God. The people whom we look to today to give us balance, to help us assess if we measure up, and to give direction can equally replace God's role within our lives. When the Monster of Comparison gets us to replace God with people, it leads to an unhealthy existence.

A religious leader of Jesus's day stood in the temple, exalting himself, saying:

> God, I thank you that I am not like other people: thieves, rogues, adulterers, or even like this tax collector. I fast twice a week; I give a tenth of all my income. (Luke 18:11–12)

Imagine the healthiest person you know, someone who is rooted in prayer and godly community. Can you imagine that person saying this prayer?

No, because no healthy person would ever need to brag like that in a prayer.

A telltale sign of unhealth is when my self-worth is determined by someone else's distance from me. If I can only lift myself up by pushing someone else down, it's because I've curved inward on myself and no longer live the life my Creator intends for me.

The Swiss philosopher Alain de Botton writes:

> The attentions of others matter to us because we are afflicted by a congenital uncertainty as to our own value, as a result of which affliction we tend to allow others' appraisals to play a determining role in how we see ourselves. Our sense of identity is held captive by the judgments of those we live among.[4]

When the Monster of Comparison has had its way with us, its pull contorts us into people who have forgotten who we are uniquely created to be.

PARROTS

As a kid, I wanted a parrot. But parrots are expensive. My parents once purchased a girl's jacket, removed the female label, and then gave the jacket to me because it was cheaper than buying me a boy's coat. So there's no way they would spend hundreds of dollars on a parrot.

Instead, my parents bought me a female parakeet, which is like Mr. Pibb to Dr Pepper, a cheap knockoff that only takes a second for you to realize is not the original. A parakeet is a small parrot, except a female parakeet doesn't do the cool thing a parrot does—it can't repeat human words.

The one bright side was that my dad couldn't train the parakeet to say, "Luke, I am your father."

One theory as to why parrots vocalize Star Wars puns or express their need for a cracker is that when parrots join a new "herd," they mimic what they hear in order to integrate. In the wild, parrots form a dialect to socially interact (like whales and dolphins). Some believe they lose this skill or never develop it when living as pets.

Maybe it is fair to say that pet parrots never hear their true voice because they are mimicking the voices around them. It is definitely fair to say that many of us never hear our true voice because we are too focused on mimicking the voices around us. Our mimicry of our idols creates insecurity and prevents us from being who we were created to be.

5.3 THE POINT

A Stable Scale

IMPRISONED

I had a college roommate. We will call him David.

Because that's what his parents named him.

David felt the need to acquire steroids. Using the reasoning skills that would eventually enable him to graduate from law school, he decided his best means to acquire steroids would be a trip across the border to a Mexican pharmacy.

David made the trip down to a border town with a non-steroid-wanting friend, who for the record was not named Luke. He parked his car on the Texas side, then the two of them walked across the border into a pharmacia where he purchased his PEDs.

David's a smart guy, albeit not smart enough to know this was a dumb idea, but still smart enough to know that it would look suspicious if he walked back across the border with syringes sticking out of his back pocket. To remedy this problem, he came up with the common solution that many men do when facing a variety of problems.

Duct tape.

After purchasing a roll of duct tape, David removed his shirt in a bathroom and began taping the syringes across his chest. His friend, finding humor in David's foray into the life of a drug mule, drew arrows across David's chest and the words "steroids here."

With the taping and temporary tattooing complete, David put on his shirt to cover the contraband, and now the two were ready to cross the border: one as an upstanding American citizen returning home and the other as a first-time drug smuggler.

But one issue remained:

What to do with the recently purchased duct tape.

David, being a God-fearing man, didn't want to do the unthinkable and discard a perfectly good roll of duct tape. So instead he walked to the border holding a partially used roll of duct tape.

He assumed the border patrol would let him and his duct tape walk across the border into Texas where he could begin his enhanced muscular development program.

He assumed wrong.

The border patrol's attention stuck to the gringo with the partially used roll of duct tape, leading to a pat down that quickly revealed the rest of the duct tape and the syringes and the writing, which gave the border patrol a nice laugh.

And that's how my college roommate ended up in a border town jail.

David used his one phone call to inform his father that his son had been incarcerated.

To which his father said,

"Son, I have a tee time in the morning. I will drive down to get you when I'm done on the golf course."

After David waited all night and through much of the next day in jail, his father bailed him out.

He said nothing to David the entire trip from Mexico to Oklahoma.

Once they were back home, his father finally decided to speak by asking him some questions.

"Have you forgotten what your last name is?"

"Have you forgotten who your grandfather is?"

"Have you forgotten whose son you are?"

"Have you forgotten who you are?"

I don't know why David wanted steroids, nor do I know why every steroid user uses them. But I do know that when we feel our identity is based on how big or strong or successful we are compared to the people around us, we lose our own unique voice and we forget who we actually are. The more time we spend on the sliding scale of comparison, the more lost we get, because we forget who we are.

WHY PROUD?

LIKE A JENGA TOWER with seconds remaining of its life, I flailed in a single-legged balancing pose in the back row of a yoga class. My instructor walked by and whispered, "Find your drishti, your stable spot on the floor, and stare at it."

As anyone who's ever tried balancing on one foot while looking at a moving object knows, it's easy to lose your balance when looking for stability from something that's not constant. But when you have your drishti, your unmoving focal point, it can give even the most unstable person a chance not to fall. Its balance and stability can become your balance and stability.

My father-in-law and I joined twenty thousand fans filling the track stadium at the University of Texas to watch the best high school track athletes compete at the state championship meet. The man in the Los Angeles Lakers tracksuit sat two rows in front of us. Somehow, his bright purple and gold attire wasn't the loudest thing about him.

During the four-by-two-hundred-meter relay finals, Mr. Purple and Gold goes from normal cheering to jumping and hysterically yelling during the anchor leg. Minimal deductive reasoning enabled me to figure out that the athlete was Mr. Purple and Gold's son.

When his son crosses the line, Mr. Purple and Gold turns around, unzips his jacket, reaches inside, and pulls out a gold medal. A medal that I am 99 percent certain was his son's from winning the two-hundred-meter open the day before. Mr. Purple and Gold puts the medal in between his teeth while he shakes his head like a dog holding a bone.

Displaying the lung capacity that enabled his son's athletic prowess, he begins yelling (with gold medal still in his mouth) for everyone in the stadium to hear:

That's my boy!

That's my boy!

That's my boy!

At the beginning of Jesus's ministry, Jesus's cousin John baptizes him. As Jesus comes up out of the water, a voice from the heavens says, "This is my Son, the Beloved, with whom I am well pleased" (Matt. 3:17).

As Jesus rises from the water, the heavenly parent shouts to anyone and everyone:

That's my boy!

When God tells Jesus and everyone around "This is my Son, the Beloved, with whom I am well pleased," what had Jesus accomplished at this point in his life?

Nothing.

He hadn't walked on water.

He hadn't preached the Sermon on the Mount.

He hadn't miraculously fed five thousand people.

He hadn't resisted the devil's temptations in the desert.

Before Jesus proves himself to be a better teacher of Torah than other rabbis, before he inspires more loyalty to his movement than other messianic figures, before he performs better miracles than other Jewish prophets, God says,

That's my boy.

Following the example of how my parents expressed their pride in me, I attempt to daily tell my daughters that I'm proud of them. Even if I say those words every day of my life, I will still have expressed only a fraction of the abiding gladness I feel in my soul for being graced with the honor of being their father.

Once, after I said "I'm proud of you" to one of my daughters when she was five, she replied, "Daddy, why are you proud of me? What have I done?"

Five rotations around the sun was long enough for her to acquire the attitude that value is based on achievement or accomplishment. It's almost as if with every rotation around the sun, we become more distant from the intrinsic worth our Creator instilled in us. We get pulled into believing our identity is tied to how we stack up to those around us instead of the blessing God has already given to us. We get pulled into thinking that only if we run faster than everyone else on the playground, or in the stadium, will we merit this love.

It doesn't have to be this way.

LISTEN

THE INVITATION of the Monster of Comparison is for you to be aware of the emptiness of the comparison game, the inequality of the sliding scale, so you will stop parroting the voices around you and be quiet enough for long enough to hear the voice that speaks to you,

the current version of you,

before you keep up with anyone,

before you master your life,

before you get your life perfected,

and says,

That's my child, with whom I'm well pleased.

It has nothing to do with what you've done. It's simply because of who you are. As Henri Nouwen says, "The real 'work' of prayer is to become silent and listen to the voice that says good things about me."[5]

The lie is that we are what others say about us or how we compare to them. The pull is to get our identity resting on that ever-sliding scale, but the point of the Monster of Comparison is that we need something better, something that God has already given to us. The invitation is to be silent and listen to what God says about us and then to trust that God's words are the truest things about us.

If we befriend the Monster of Comparison, we will see the warning that our eyes can't be fixed on what's seen but only on the One whose love for us and pleasure in us is the same yesterday, today, and forever.

NOT FAIR

THE DUTCH PRIMATOLOGIST FRANS DE WAAL, in his famous study on equality, trained Capuchin monkeys to use stones as currency.[6] For one stone the monkeys received one slice of cucumber. The stone-to-cucumber economy made for happy participants until the arrival of a grape, which threw a monkey wrench in it.*

Two monkeys trained in this economy approached a trainer at the front of their cage to participate in their regular transaction. The first monkey participant gave a stone and happily received a cucumber slice. The second monkey participant also gave a stone but received a grape. Upon seeing the second participant's reward, the first participant became furious, banging on the floor and then throwing the cucumber out of the cage. Participant one wasn't having this unfair monkey business.†

At the root of comparison is an inability to accept the inequitable allocations of blessings and resources in our unfair world. When we see that someone else received a better meal, a better salary, a better response, more adoration, it makes us unappreciative of what we have. Yet there will always be an inequitable distribution of blessings because life is not fair.

We've all been created in the image of God, but there were only a dozen who got to be among Jesus's twelve disciples. Others may have wanted to be in the inner circle but instead drew the short straw.

We've all been fearfully and wonderfully made, but some get ten talents, some five talents, and others only one talent.

---

*Sorry. I'm not proud of that joke either, but it's also not my worst pun, even in this story.

†There it is.

We've all been impressed with the divine likeness, but some will have more likable jobs, healthier families, and larger social media followings.

We've all been given the designation of being ministers of reconciliation, but only a handful of preachers will lead churches that grow numerically from two hundred to ten thousand.

Like the Capuchin monkey, we can't stomach the capricious distribution of long straws because we've got problems with inequality. God doesn't seem concerned enough to always eradicate the inequitable allocation of talents and resources, not even with the first set of brothers, Cain and Abel. Each brought God an offering: Cain's from the fruit of the ground and Abel's from the firstlings of the sheep. God favored Abel over Cain for reasons the book of Genesis doesn't provide. God didn't resolve the tension. Not only did God not resolve the tension but also God might have done more than just allow the tension.

Old Testament scholar Walter Brueggemann says about God (Yahweh):

> Essential to the plot is the capricious freedom of Yahweh. Like the narrator, we must resist every effort to explain it. There is nothing here of Yahweh preferring cowboys to farmers. There is nothing here to disqualify Cain. . . . The family would perhaps have gotten along better without this God. But he is there. All through the Genesis narratives, Yahweh is there to disrupt, to create tensions, and to evoke the shadowy side of reality.[7]

While Hebrews[8] seems to have an explanation, Genesis doesn't care to resolve the tension of why God preferred Abel to Cain; the only care is how Cain responds to life being unfair. The concern isn't the presence of inequality, it's how we respond to inequality.[9]

The world will always be unstable in its allocation of resources, talents, and gifts. If you chase the prop, you will seek to acquire more than the people around you because you've forgotten your identity on comparison's sliding scale. But if you get the point, you will see the need to be grounded in divine love. Then you can live authentically with your voice in your lane.

5.4 THE LIGHT

Your Lane

NOW A PARABLE as told by my friend Wade Hodges.

> Once upon a time three kids found a bag of walnuts and took it to the wisest man in their village. They asked him to divide the nuts among them as God would.
>
> So the sage gave the first kid one walnut.
>
> To the second he gave five walnuts.
>
> Then he gave the rest, well over fifty walnuts, to the third.
>
> The first two protested, "That's not fair!"
>
> The sage said, "You didn't ask me to be fair. You asked me to distribute them as God would."
>
> The third kid, the one who was holding the bag of walnuts, asked the sage, "Why did you give me so much more than the others?"
>
> "Wrong question," said the sage.
>
> Burdened by the responsibility he was holding in his hands, the third kid said, "I agree with the others. This isn't fair."
>
> The sage said, "Why are you complaining to me about what is unfair, when you're the one with all the walnuts?"
>
> The sage turned and walked away.
>
> The third kid called after him, "What am I going to do with all these walnuts?"
>
> The sage smiled and said over his shoulder, "Now that is the right question."[10]

Most of us will never understand why God blesses some with more talents than us, just like we will never understand why we've been gifted with more talents than others. No matter how we compare our lot to others, there will always be disparity. Focusing on differences only distances us from where God wants us to focus and what we were created to be.

At the end of John's Gospel, Jesus tells Peter that his life will be taken from him. Peter then looks over his shoulder at John and asks a reasonable question: "Lord, what about him?"

Jesus responds, "If it is my will that he remain until I come, what is that to you? Follow me!"[11]

Sure, Peter, your life might be taken from you while the guy-next-to-you's life isn't, but what is that to you?

In the 2016 Olympic final of the two-hundred-meter butterfly, South African swimmer Chad le Clos, the 2012 gold medalist in the event, swam next to the most accomplished swimmer in Olympic history, Michael Phelps. A daunting task for Chad le Close, even though he had bested Phelps in the same race four years before.

Toward the race's conclusion, a picture of le Clos was taken that would go viral. Chad le Clos looks over his shoulder and out of his lane to see Phelps a full length ahead of him. Phelps, who won the race, stared directly at his destination, paying no attention to the lane next to him.

Looking at the lane next to us almost never helps us get to where we need to go or become who we could be. When we peer into someone else's lane and ask what about them, the divine response continues to be, "What is that to you? Follow me!"

With the Monster of Comparison, the light gets in by getting us to see our lane, our life, and our lot as our place to manifest the love we've received from God.

The Torah says, "You shall not covet your neighbor's house; you shall not covet your neighbor's wife, or male or female slave, or ox, or donkey, or anything that belongs to your neighbor" (Exod. 20:17).

Covet is essentially the Old Testament word for comparison. The Ten Commandments describe coveting in the context of craving your neighbor's possessions, but it's not your neighbor that coveting truly offends. Coveting offends not the one who possesses the ox or the donkey but the One who gave both you and your neighbor all that you possess. It's a mockery of the giver because it's a dissatisfaction with the lane your Creator has assigned you to.

My comparison was never about Matt as a person; Matt was simply a prop. If I had been in a different setting in a different town, it would have been a different person. Just as coveting wasn't ultimately about the neighbor's ox or donkey. Comparison isn't about how we relate to others; it's about how we relate to God. The point of the Monster of Comparison is that lanes will not always be equal, but if you befriend this monster, you learn to hear what the *true* voice says about you. Then you can remove yourself from the sliding scale and thrive in whatever lane you've been given.

There's a famous story about Rabbi Zusya while he was on his deathbed. His student, noticing Rabbi Zusya's sad demeanor, asked, "Rabbi, why are you so sad? After all the great things you have accomplished, your place in heaven is assured!"

"I'm afraid!" Zusya replied. "Because when I get to heaven, God won't ask me 'Why weren't you more like Moses?' or 'Why weren't you more like King David?' God will ask, 'Zusya, why weren't you more like Zusya?'"[12]

6

More

6.1 THE PROP
I Need More

DUMBLIFT

IN FIVE HOURS, I will board a flight to Chicago to meet up with my friend Jason for the first part of a two-week stretch of travel that will take me from Austin to Chicago, South Bend, Paris, Tel Aviv, Jerusalem, Palestine, and, of course, Nashville. But now, I'm in my favorite room and the only room where I have sovereignty in my own house:

my garage gym.

For the record, I've only been assigned control of half of the garage, but nevertheless, it's my favorite half of a room in my house.

I've completed my standard thirty minutes of yoga and mobility warm-up before I begin my last workout in my garage gym for the next two weeks. And yes, my standard preworkout warm-up takes thirty minutes because I'm not twenty anymore.

Today I will be performing the deadlift—an exercise lacking in subtlety of name or complexity of movement. One simply bends over, picks up a barbell from the ground, and stands up. Over the next fifteen minutes, I will increase the weight on the bar in twenty- to thirty-pound increments until reaching a weight that I'm able to lift only two or three times.

My back, hamstrings, and hips all feel loose, a feeling that doesn't happen by accident anymore. Feeling great turns into feeling confident,

125

which turns into feeling risky enough to keep adding more and more weight.

A voice in my head says to quit while I'm ahead, because the last thing I want is to be stuck on an airplane or in an unfamiliar bed with a sore back.

But what's the fun in being responsible?

I add another twenty pounds to the bar, bringing the total to the highest weight I've attempted to deadlift in four years. The voice of reason tries to interject, so I crank up my music.

The following is the actual conversation I have with myself:

The smart thing is to stop while we are ahead, but when have we ever been accused of being smart?

Pay no attention to the plural pronoun used in my self-talk. That's our business, not yours.

But do pay attention to us saying that we aren't smart.

As I approach the bar, my four-year-old daughter walks into the garage. I love having my girls join me in the garage, so we have diminutive camping chairs available for them on the opposite side of the garage in the non-Luke territory.

I grip the bar in the standard deadlift over-under grip, left hand under the bar, right hand over the bar, slightly wider than shoulder width. I roll the bar back toward my shins—chest out, core tight—push my feet into the ground, and pull the bar. It comes off the ground easily. The bar travels halfway up. My confidence is sky-high.

Suddenly my posture disintegrates.

My abs collapse, my hips fly backward. All the strain then dumps on my now unprotected lower back.

My back buckles.

I am like one of Cupid's victims as an arrow of pain shoots into my lower lumbar.

I drop the weight and my verbal standards. I crumble to the ground while my four-year-old tries to process the unfamiliar word she has just heard.

I roll onto my side and think,

We are an idiot.

Why couldn't a safe and conservative final workout before two weeks of traveling be good enough?

Why did I need just a little more?

Why couldn't what I had be enough?

My quest for more left my back hurting for the next week and my friend Jason carrying my bags. It's not the first time my quest for more has hurt me and caused those around me to carry the weight of my decisions.

MORE

IN THE SECOND CREATION STORY OF GENESIS, after animating dust into the man, Adam, with God's own breath, God plants a delightful garden in Eden with every tree pleasing to the eye and tasteful to the tongue. Adam and the soon-to-be-created Eve can have fruit from every tree save one—the tree of the knowledge of good and evil.

Along comes a crafty snake. The innocence of Adam and Eve was no match for the cunning creature. With a simple twist of the words of God, the snake's temptation to eat from the one prohibited tree was too great for them.

Adam and Eve's decision fractured their relationship and all future creations' relationships with the Creator for one simple reason: every tree minus one wasn't enough.

They wanted more.

We. Want. More.

As Henri Nouwen said, one of the three lies we are tempted to believe is that we are what we have. When we are what we have, the crafty voice of temptation will always say that we don't have enough. We might have an entire garden at our fingertips, but if there's one tree that's off limits, something within us wishes that we had just one more.

Despite all the evidence to the contrary, despite all the examples of people who have tasted of that tree yet still hunger for more, we still genuinely believe if we were the ones who had a bite from that tree, we would be full.

If I had

that house,

that job,

that bank account,

that accolade,

that appearance,

that achievement,

that experience,

then, and only then, will I be full.

It's the archetypal story that's been told from the beginning. Even if we have an entire garden full of trees, the trees that we have aren't enough. We always feel the need for more. And in our pursuit for more, we end up with less. We will make comments such as "I deserve to be happy" and then devour things that lead to heartbreak. We will go to the extreme to acquire and consume facets of the human experience to excessive levels with disregard for how, in our quest for more, we end up being consumed.

Ever since the garden of Eden, the Monster of More has tricked us into thinking that we need more—more power, more money, more sex, more pleasure, more food, more respect, more followers. So we chase after the prop of the Monster of More, disregarding the side effects that will follow.

HUNGRY MUNGRY

IN SHEL SILVERSTEIN'S EPONYMOUS POEM "Hungry Mungry," the monster Mungry sits at a table with his parents while he consumes a meal that would feed an entire football team. The food runs out but his appetite doesn't. When the food disappears, he starts eating the table. Mom and Dad think this is a bit much, so they tell their son to stop.

Mungry thinks that advice is a bit much, so he eats his folks.

Then he eats his house, his neighbors, the police, the army, the United States, the Egyptian pyramids, the church in Rome, the grass in Africa, and then the whole world, and for dessert he eats the universe. When left with nothing else, Mungry starts eating his own feet, then legs, hips, and neck, and finally his lips. "Till he sat there just gnashin' his teeth, 'cause nothin' was nothin' was . . . nothin' was left to eat."[1]

Our delightful garden doesn't seem delightful enough because it's lacking one tree, so we go looking for more. The intoxication of more leaves us like Mungry, consuming ourselves.

6.2 THE PULL

Never Enough

FINDS A WAY

IN THE ORIGINAL *JURASSIC PARK* MOVIE, the following conversation takes place as the scientists flee from velociraptors:

"Are you sure the third one is contained?" Dr. Alan Grant asks.

Dr. Ellie Sattler replies with some amazing foreshadowing: "Yes, unless they figure out how to open doors."

Unless they figure out how to open doors.

That's what we call foreshadowing.

I wonder if the velociraptors will ever figure it out?

Of course they'll figure it out because monsters always morph, evolve, and adapt. The velociraptors learn not only how to open doors but also how to breed, even though all the animals in the park are genetically conditioned to be female.

Here's another scene from *Jurassic Park* in which the improbability of female dinosaurs breeding is discussed.

Dr. Ian Malcolm says, "John, the kind of control you're attempting simply is . . . it's not possible. If there is one thing the history of evolution has taught us it's that life will not be contained. Life breaks free, it expands to new territories and crashes through barriers, painfully, maybe even dangerously, but, uh . . . well, there it is."

John Hammond says sarcastically, "There it is."

Henry Wu says, "You're implying that a group composed entirely of female animals will . . . breed?"

Dr. Malcolm says, "No. I'm, I'm simply saying that life, uh . . . finds a way."[2]

If we, the viewers of *Jurassic Park*, already believe that people have created dinosaurs by finding their blood within mosquitoes fossilized in amber, and if we also believe that someone has turned said dinosaurs into attractions at an oversized zoo on an island, then there's no way we won't go along with the idea that dinosaurs can switch genders.

The idea of a dinosaur switching gender compared to the entire premise of the movie is not that unbelievable because if we know anything about monsters, it's that they never stay the same, they always adapt. Monsters always find a way to continue to haunt us, especially the Monster of More.

ADAPTATION

THE WORST THING TO EVER HAPPEN to my podcast was a graph. When I started my podcast back in the podcasting dark ages before almost everyone had a podcast, I didn't realize that one could track how many people listened. Weeks after starting my podcast, I was on my host's website when I stumbled upon a graphic depicting my listeners.

The graph showed how many days of the previous thirty days didn't reach a thousand downloads, which was all of them, as each day was a futile effort to summit the top of the graph. After first seeing this graph, I couldn't stop looking at it. Each day, I hoped it would reach that magic mark of one thousand downloads per day.

One day, after having over five hundred downloads by midmorning, I knew that day would be the day I reached the pinnacle of podcasting—one thousand downloads in a day. I assumed once I reached a thousand, the graph would break, the internet would shut down, and I would be crowned the Patron Saint of Podcasting.

I reached the threshold by late afternoon, but instead of the graphic breaking, it was my hopes and dreams that broke as the graph recalibrated from a one-thousand-listen scale to a five-thousand-listen scale.

And the cycle started all over again. Every time a goal was reached, the Monster of More recalibrated and created a new one.

That's how the brain works too.

Because of the limited nature of happiness, we often think the limiter of happiness comes from our wallets. We think that if we had more money, we would have more happiness. But research has shown that the countries with the highest happiness rates are surprisingly not the richest countries.

The real enemy of happiness isn't our bank accounts but our brains. Jonathan Haidt spells this out in his book *The Happiness Hypothesis* when he makes the point that the brain isn't sensitive to absolute levels but rather to elevations and depressions.[3] When something good happens, like a pay raise, your happiness increases because you now can afford a Jet Ski and a Hawaiian vacation. But the brain doesn't say, "I am now always going to be happy because I have a Jet Ski in my garage and Hawaiian vacation pictures on my Instagram."

Instead, in what he calls the adaptation principle, Haidt argues that the brain adapts to this financial elevation as a new absolute level, a new normal. The initial novelty of leaving the old non-Jet-Ski-and-non-Hawaiian-vacation level and going into the new Jet-Ski-and-Hawaiian-vacation level caused a spike in happiness because the brain is acutely aware of the change. However, once this change becomes your new normal, your happiness regresses to the baseline degree of happiness pre-raise. This is why on December 27th, kids are typically just as happy as they were on December 24th. They may now have all the toys they had been dreaming of for the last month, but their brain in that brief period of time has adapted to their post-Christmas toy level after two days (or less) of new-toy-induced bliss. The by-product of the elevation change—happiness—doesn't last because our mind, an amazingly adaptive computer, has adjusted to the new normal.

On the shoulders of two other research projects, Haidt argues that lottery winners and those who suffer injuries causing them to become paraplegics return within a year to very similar baseline degrees of happiness as they had before winning the lottery or suffering the injury. The initial few months after the changes are drastically different, but people don't stay there because their minds are busy adapting to their new normals. Both groups might now be living in different levels, but their brains have adapted to them as new absolute levels.

As soon as you get a bite of the fruit of that last tree, another tree appears.

Just when you think you've squelched the Monster of More, it mutates. The pull of the Monster of More makes what we now have never enough because it always mutates and always asks for more.

A few years back, I'm listening to a podcast on my earbuds while mowing my backyard when a ringtone comes through.

I stop the mower and answer.

"Luke, what are you doing?" Wade asks.

"Mowing."

"I've got floor seats for the Mavs, VIP passes, and platinum parking. You interested?"

"Wade, you had me at floor seats."

"Ok, Luke, you need to leave five minutes ago."

"But I'm mowing—never mind, Wade. I will pick you up in a few."

So I just up and leave. Yard half-mowed, lawn mower sitting in the middle of the lawn, Weed eater leaning up against the fence. My backyard looked as if the rapture had just occurred.

Minutes later, Wade sits in my truck and we drive into the platinum parking area of the Dallas Mavericks' arena. Instead of the usual mile-long walk from a distant parking lot through an overcrowded entrance, I park my ten-year-old truck next to an assortment of Ferraris and Lamborghinis and then take a few short steps into the arena through a private door. Before going to our seats, we make our way into the VIP section for a pregame meal where I stand in line waiting to get salmon and steak next to Super Bowl–winning quarterback Russell Wilson. Then finally we walk out of the VIP section onto the actual court to make our way to our seats.

No longer am I walking on the sticky floors of the nosebleed sections to get to my seat. Today, I walk on the actual hardwood just like I am Mavs legend Dirk Nowitizki, albeit a pocket-sized version.

Years later I know that answering that phone call while mowing my yard has ruined all basketball games for me forever, because I can't un-see and un-experience the good life.

So to recap.

Could I afford the platinum parking, VIP passes, or floor seats?

No.

Could my friend afford those seats?

No.

Could I ever again enjoy another Mavs game where I have to park a mile away and then eat a hot dog in a normal seat like a peasant?

No.

My mind has been attacked by the Monster of More through the adaptation principle.

Solomon says in Proverbs 23:1–3:

> When you sit down to eat with a ruler,
>   observe carefully what is before you,
> and put a knife to your throat
>   if you have a big appetite.
> Do not desire the ruler's delicacies,
>   for they are deceptive food.

Why does Solomon think that you should put a knife to your throat?

Maybe because Solomon knew that you would get accustomed to the king's table and no longer appreciate your table. No matter how much you feed the brain with the ruler's delicacies, deadlift or podcasting goals, Jet Skis, Hawaiian vacations, or VIP passes, the brain works faster to adapt, making happiness the Road Runner to our Wile E. Coyote. Just when you think you have happiness caught, happiness breaks free—because nothing from the outside can cure the wound within us.

6.3 THE POINT
Never Full

JEPHTHAH

LET ME TELL YOU AN ATROCIOUS STORY from an atrocious section of Scripture known as the book of Judges. The larger narrative of the book of Judges shows Israel's downward spiral as a nation, revealing Israel's need of a new leadership structure. Judges lays the foundation for the implementation of Israel's monarchy and their first king, Saul.

One of the predecessors of the kings, a military man named Jephthah, led the Israelites in battle against the Ammonites after promising God that if they win he will sacrifice whatever (or possibly "whoever" as the Hebrew is unclear) the first thing is that greets him when he returns home. Given the typical design of an ancient courtyard with domesticated animals, Jephthah might have intended to offer livestock from his courtyard, but an animal was not what first greeted him.

A victorious Jephthah returns home to his only child coming out to meet him. She is dancing with timbrels, celebrating her victorious father's return home.

Jephthah tears his clothes and weeps.

After he informs her of the situation, she accepts her fate but first asks for time to go into the wilderness to mourn her virginity for two months. After which she returned to her father, "who did with her according to the vow he had made."[4]

About this atrocious story, Fr. Ronald Rolheiser writes:

> There's a rather nasty patriarchal character to this story (such were the times) and, of course, we are right to abhor the very idea of human sacrifice. . . . What do death and virginity mean in this story?
>
> They're metaphors inside a parable meant to teach a profound truth—namely, all of us, no matter what age or state in life, must at some point mourn what's incomplete and not consummated in our lives. . . .
>
> In the end, like her, we all die virgins, having lived incomplete lives, not having achieved the intimacy we craved, and having yearned to create a lot more things than we were able to birth. In this life, nobody gets the full symphony. There's a place inside us where we all "bewail our virginity," and this is true too of married people, just as it is of celibates. At some deep level on this side of eternity, we all sleep alone.[5]

Within everyone exists an incomplete and unconsummated facet of our soul because none of us get the "full symphony." Not because we can't acquire enough but because in this age we were never intended to be full. The cycle of attraction, acquisition, and adaptation futilely repeats itself, not because of a flaw in assessing our wants but because of an ignorance of the cracked human experience.

Jephthah's daughter mourns her unfulfilled desire to be a mother. Some of us join her in mourning for a family that we desire but never receive. Some of us mourn the loss of our own victories outside the home that we never experience. But for every one of us, there's a part of life that doesn't ever become what we've craved for it to be.

CRACKED

WHEN I WAS A TEN-YEAR-OLD, my parents didn't give me a parrot but they did give me an aquarium—in my second-story bedroom. Filling this aquarium required the involvement of the entire family, except for my redheaded brother.

My dad threw a water hose from the flowerbed to my second-story bedroom window. Upon catching the hose, I placed it into the empty aquarium. My dad walked upstairs while my mom manned the flowerbed's faucet on the ground level.

My mother turned on the faucet while my father held the hose in the aquarium.

My redheaded brother roamed around upstairs, being useless.

As the water halfway filled the aquarium, my dad's trust in me reached the point at which he assumed I could be left alone to hold the hose in the aquarium.

He assumed wrong.

After he left the room, I almost immediately began placing fish into their half-full new home while the water continued to rush in through the hose. The fish seemed to enjoy being spun around rapidly by the hose, just like surfers seem to enjoy being sucked under by a wave after crashing.

Next, I decided to add the decorative rocks because, as the Bible probably should say somewhere, "It's not good for fish to be alone."

I gently placed the first rock on the bottom of the aquarium. But one rock wasn't enough. Just as my hand, holding the second rock, hovered above the aquarium, my father walked back into the room. I dropped the rock as fear washed over me.

Which is exactly what the water did to my feet after the rock hit the bottom of the aquarium.

My dad, filled with the superhuman strength given to fathers when someone is wasting something in their home, ran like Usain Bolt to grab the hose, which was now pouring water through the cracked aquarium into my bedroom. He threw the hose out the second-story window, where it landed on the unsuspecting head of my mother. She, like the rock in the aquarium, crashed to the ground with what we would now call a concussion.

Upstairs, I'm terrified because my fish are now flopping on the floor, so I'm on my hands and knees trying to find Nemo. Downstairs, water was leaking through light fixtures. My dad frantically tried to find towels to soak up the gallons and gallons of water. My mother remained concussed in the flowerbed. All the while, my redheaded brother is having the time of his life, running up and down the hallway yelling like a pirate,

"Abandon ship, matey!!! She's taking on water."

No amount of water would fill my cracked aquarium.

My dad didn't think water of the right temperature or from the right bottle would fill it. My dad knew what many of us never acknowledge. Because a crack exists, so does incompleteness. No substance, regardless of value or quality, will fill the void. Since a crack is present, there will always be an inability for our lives to be full.

The pull from the Monster of More is to think that we need to grasp for something to fill our hearts, but the point of the Monster of More is for us to see that the emptiness will always exist. The point is that the crack was included in our creation.

NEVER FULL

As the German philosopher Walter Benjamin said, we are cracked vessels.[6] No matter how many trees we have, no matter how many VIP passes or meals at the king's table, no matter how much is poured into us, we will never be full.

In Plato's *Symposium*, the Greek playwright Aristophanes says that humans were originally four-armed and four-legged creatures with a completely round head with two faces and four ears. These powerful creatures threatened the scale of the heavens, so the gods cut them in half, leveling the playing field between the gods and humanity while also forever creating an unfulfilled yearning for wholeness in humanity.

The writer of Ecclesiastes in a moment of disillusion writes:

> Whatever my eyes desired I did not keep from them; I kept my heart from no pleasure, for my heart found pleasure in all my toil, and this was my reward for all my toil. Then I considered all that my hands had done and the toil I had spent in doing it, and again, all was vanity and a chasing after wind, and there was nothing to be gained under the sun. (2:10–11)

It's the vanity of filling a cracked jar and the futility of chasing after the wind. Harvard psychologist Daniel Gilbert says it this way:

> In short, the production of wealth does not necessarily make individuals happy, but it does serve the needs of an economy which serves the needs of a stable society, which serves as a network for the propagation of delusional beliefs about happiness and wealth.[7]

The Monster of More is behind these delusional beliefs about happiness and wealth.

The Monster of More is behind the affair, selling you ecstasy with the forbidden sexual experience.

The Monster of More is behind the justification that you deserve that extravagant spending.

The Monster of More tells you that you aren't full yet, so you need to take more.

But if we befriend the Monster of More, we realize that we aren't meant to be full. Just as the serpent twisted the words of God in the garden, we can twist the words of the Monster of More by acknowledging their half-truth. We aren't full, but we were never meant to be full.

The Monster of More says that what we need is just around the corner or behind the currently inaccessible door. The truth no one wants to say but everyone needs to hear is that in this age we will always have an unsatisfied craving. The Christian story tells us that we are groaning, waiting for redemption, a redemption that can't be found in any of this age's trees. If we befriend the Monster of More, we learn that we are cracked and thus will never be full here. And that's when the saving light comes in, to show us that the symphony's beauty is in its incompleteness.

6.4 THE LIGHT
Gifted

SNUGGIE

My brother once gave me a Snuggie for Christmas. A gift that I am almost certain was either a regift or found in a trash can. If you don't know what a Snuggie is, lucky you, because it's the Frankenstein's monster of bedding. It's an ungodly mixture of a blanket and a sweatshirt that the book of Leviticus would surely have condemned.

Once back home from my family's Christmas, I had to put the mutant blanket somewhere, since throwing a Christmas present away immediately would be uncouth. I placed the Snuggie, still in its plastic bag, behind the reading chair in my home office.

A few fateful days later, while reading in my office, a winter's breeze chilled my body. In a moment of frigid desperation, I did the unthinkable: I let Frankenstein's monster out of the bag. With the blanket part covering my body, I reluctantly slid my arms through the sleeves, and shamefully placed my phone in the pocket.

Like Adam in the garden after eating the forbidden fruit, my eyes were opened to a whole new world. The Snuggie provided the warmth of a blanket with the functionality of a sweatshirt.

Would I have ever bought one for myself?

Absolutely not.

But have I continued to use it since then?

Absolutely.

I never would have spent my own money to buy a Snuggie, but since it had been gifted to me, I experienced it differently.

When receiving something as a gift, we don't have expectations or demands for what it's supposed to do. We don't demand that it meet a certain need or live up to a specific standard of quality. Instead, we can receive and appreciate the gift without expectations.

When you buy a house, you examine the home for flaws and faults. You get a market comparison to determine the appropriate dollar figure for the house. You likely hire an inspector to professionally nitpick every last imperfection of the house. You do all these things because you are spending a substantial amount of money and you want to ensure that you get exactly what you feel entitled to.

How much different would you act if someone gave you that exact same house as a gift? Would you feel the need to check the market value before you decided to accept it? No, you simply would receive it without critique or analysis because you didn't deserve it, you weren't owed it, and you didn't work for it.

Because it was a gift, you would treat it differently.

When we stop demanding relationships, possessions, and honors to fill a void, we turn our greedy grasping-for-more hands into palms-open receptive hands that receive all of life as a gift. The difference between grasping and receiving may seem subtle, but the outcome couldn't be more drastic.

You weren't made to be redeemed in this age. You weren't promised to be full. You weren't offered a carefree life with no obstacles. The Monster of More makes you fully aware of that. But if you can baptize that, the incompleteness becomes a reminder that being full was never something you were promised. So whatever you do receive can be experienced as a gift, an undeserved grace.

GOD'S WILL

"GIVE THANKS IN ALL CIRCUMSTANCES; for this is the will of God in Christ Jesus for you" (1 Thess. 5:18).

God's will for you is less about where you go, what you do, and when you do it and more about who you are. God's will is less about making sure you go down a mysterious, singular right path through a mythical right door, because a God who distantly watches while you try to determine the only door God wants you to walk through isn't loving. That doesn't pass the good-parent test. A good parent wouldn't do that, so of course God wouldn't do that. God's will is more about who you are through whatever door you step. And the type of person God wills for you to be is someone who has gratitude in all circumstances.

Despite this being your Creator's desire for you, this grateful disposition doesn't happen without practice. As Brené Brown said,

> [I] never talk about gratitude and joy separately, for this reason. In twelve years, I've never interviewed a single person who would describe their lives as joyful, who would describe themselves as joyous, who was not actively practicing gratitude.[8]

I love the phrase "practicing gratitude" because in a world so influenced by the Monster of More, gratitude doesn't happen without effort. Our culture has been consumed by the lie of consumption, so practicing gratitude will always mean swimming upstream.

Just think about how we celebrate birthdays.

Imagine an alien showing up at your next birthday party. A nice, ET-like alien who is curious about the festivities, so you have to explain the birthday party phenomenon to him.

Here's how I imagine the conversation with the alien would go:

Alien: "I see, human, that you are having a party. What did you do to earn this party?"

Human: "I was born."

Alien: "What did you do to be born?"

Human: "Um . . . nothing. I was just born. That lady over there in the kitchen getting the cake ready did all the work."

Alien: "So why does she not get presents?"

Human: "Because I was the one born. That's why she buys the presents for me."

Alien: "Let me get this straight, human. She was the one who did all the work, and now she's the one who made the cake for you, which you just complained about because the cake was not the right flavor. And she also bought you presents?"

Human: "Yes, Mr. Alien, but wait, I'll explain more in a minute. We must stop, because she's also about to sing me a song."

For many of us on our birthdays, the person who gives gifts, bakes a cake, and sings to us is the person who did something—childbirth—on this day years before that, until very recently in human history, had a very good chance of killing her. She could have died for us, yet she's the one throwing us a party. And we wonder why gratitude doesn't come easy for us.

In a culture that's been consumed by the Monster of More, gratitude is like swimming upstream, but those who cultivate practices of gratitude experience the joy of living a life according to our Creator's will for us. Gratitude isn't about a deposit into our lives but a disposition to all of life. Happiness comes from a deposit, such as a Jet Ski or a Hawaiian vacation, but happiness will fade. Gratitude is the evergreen disposition to all of life that reminds us that what we have right now is enough.

POURED OUT

IN 2 SAMUEL 23, KING DAVID, parched by the dry heat of harvest time, wistfully longed for a drink of water from his hometown's well.

A nostalgic longing by an old man that cannot realistically be fulfilled because his enemies, the Philistines, are camped between him and his hometown of Bethlehem. But three of David's honor guard, after overhearing his wish, break through the Philistine's camp, get to Bethlehem, draw the water, and carry it back miles and miles to David. A shocked David refuses the drink because this unexpected act of loyalty was too great an honor for him to simply drink. In an act of respect to the three soldiers, David pours the water out as a sacred drink offering to the Lord.

Gratitude turns what we receive—the drinks, the honors, the money—into a gift given to us, not because we deserve it or because it could take our wistful longings away, but simply because our Creator has bestowed it upon us as a grace. Part of the way we honor the giver is by the practice of leaving some on the table. The Israelites had a practice known as gleaning, which left part of their fields unharvested out of concern for the alien, the stranger, the widow, and the poor. While initially it was done for the sake of others, I imagine it also became a practice that reminded them they could survive sufficiently on 90 percent of the harvest. A reminder that they don't need all of it to be always grateful.

LBJ

A YEAR AFTER THE FIRST TRIP to the basketball promised land, I got the call again. Same floor seats, VIP passes, and platinum parking, same urgent timing that required an instant response, but this time the opponent was the Miami Heat, the defending NBA champions led by LeBron James.

I told Lindsay about this once-in-a-lifetime opportunity.

She told me that this evening, December 20, was the night "we" had decided to celebrate our family Christmas before traveling to celebrate the holidays with our extended families.

So what did I do?

Did I go watch LeBron James, one of the two greatest basketball players of all time?

Or did I watch my three daughters' fleeting happiness from receiving a deposit of presents that will all be thrown away by next year?

Did I watch from inches away as LeBron James went for twenty-four points, nine rebounds, and five assists in a 110 to 95 victory over the Mavericks?

No. I stayed home.

But now, six years later, do I regret not going to the basketball game?

Yes.

Of course, I regret not going. We've opened presents every Christmas since then, but I've yet to have a chance like that to watch LeBron James. This is my family's equivalent of Leonardo DiCaprio in *Titanic* drowning in freezing cold water because Kate Winslet wouldn't scoot over and make room for him on the floating door. There was clearly room for both opening presents and sitting courtside next to LeBron.

But sometimes we don't need more, because what we have right now is already more grace than we deserve.

Sometimes we learn to leave a box unopened, a drink unconsumed, and an experience untapped because what our Creator wills for us isn't the acquisition of another deposit but the development of a grateful disposition.

7

Success

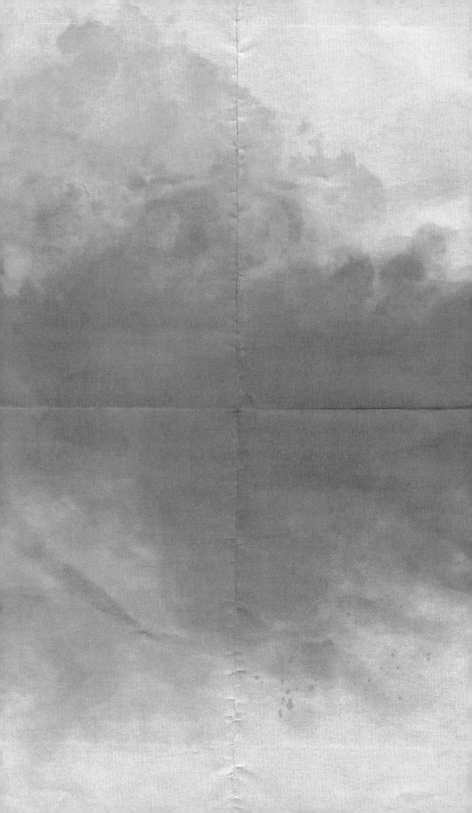

7.1 THE PROP
I Am What I Do

OHHH

Soon after becoming the speaker at Grace Bible Study, I stood in an airport boarding line next to two couples about my parents' ages. When they asked what I did for a living, I told them that I was a preacher—because I was twenty-one and hadn't yet learned that in situations like this I should obfuscate my vocation. I say *obfuscate* because when I use a fancy word, I don't feel as guilty as when I use the more direct word *lie*. It's the linguistic equivalent of a white-collar crime. I told them about Grace Bible Study, which caused them to ask the irresistible question for Americans.

"How many people attend?"

To which I proudly said,

"A thousand people."

To which the now wide-eyed foursome in unison responded,

"Ohhh."

And I liked it.

Over time, I developed the skill of leading conversations to repeat this exchange because I loved the dopamine rush. If I asked a stranger what they did for work, they would reciprocate. When I said I was a preacher, if they were American, it was a mortal lock that they would ask how many people attended—because Americans need to know if someone is in the winner's circle.

JACKET

HENRI NOUWEN SAID THAT WE ARE ALL TEMPTED to believe we are what we do. And if we are what we do, then we'd better be good at it.

Upon losing my two matches at the district wrestling tournament, ending the season in my sophomore year of high school, I had two great rewards waiting for me.

Reward one, I would consume an ungodly amount of junk food after having cut my body weight from 160 pounds to make the 135-pound weight class. Within thirty-six hours of the season ending, which included two stops at fast-food restaurants and one trip to a Pizza Hut buffet, I had gained the most satisfying dozen pounds of my life.

Reward two, my now not-so-emaciated body would be covered in the couture of a champion, the oh-so-coveted varsity jacket, the truest sign for this fifteen-year-old that he was in the winner's circle. It took eight weeks for my varsity jacket to be personalized, meaning it arrived at the same time as the spring weather.

Day one of life with said varsity jacket was forecasted to reach eighty-five degrees, but I still put on my varsity jacket that morning before leaving the house because can one ever really trust meteorologists?

After school, I sat with a group of friends on the aluminum bleachers wearing my varsity jacket and watching a track meet. Surprisingly, the weather was in the mideighties.

But was I going to take off the varsity jacket?

Of course not.

Was I drenched in sweat?

Of course.

Was I going to complain?

No.

Because, as my brother's No Fear T-shirt declared, "Pain is weakness leaving the body."

Or in this case, it was my LA Looks hair gel leaving my hair and dripping onto my face.

Despite the discomfort I was in, I wasn't going to take off my jacket because I wanted everyone (including myself) to know that I was a winner.

The brothers James and John had probably heard Jesus's teachings on "the first will be last" and "the greatest among you will be your servant." Yet these two apostles asked for the seats of authority at Jesus's right and left hands because even apostles want to be in the winner's circle.[1] While asking for seats of privilege may sound bad, those who attended a Christian summer camp that gave out the "Most Christian Camper" award don't get to judge.

The desire to be winners overrides logic.

Including the logic that believing you are what you do is a lie or the logic that being encumbered by a coat that feeds your ego but makes you sweat is a bad decision. Nevertheless, we continue to wear our own versions of a varsity jacket.

Not every jacket promotes your athletic prowess, but every jacket that makes you feel like you are in the winner's circle while also making you miserable can be your version of a varsity jacket.

My friend Yvette, an OB-GYN oncologist, once told me that her occupation creates the expectation of perfection. We all know that no human is perfect, not even a doctor, but the physician's white coat with all its prestige and social standing can make you feel as if you are unable to make a mistake or admit that you don't know something. The white coat can feel like a straitjacket that doesn't allow you to be a normal person. It might be why doctors have high burnout and suicide rates. The jacket sure looks good on and affords great opportunity to help people and to create a good life for you and your family, but it will make you sweat.

Some put on their own varsity jacket of being lovable. If that's you, then you are the kind of person who is always conscientious of others' feelings and happiness, making everyone want to be around you. Wanting to be useful and loving is an admirable motivation. Unlike many vain and selfish jackets, this one feels like a soft, fluffy jacket that everyone wants to cuddle up next to. How the Monster of Success presents itself to you is a bit harder to see. But you can tell because it will make you sweat like a teenager in a leather coat in eighty-five-degree heat. You don't need people to see you as smart or accomplished, you just need them to see you as someone they like. You do everything you can to make that happen. You will sacrifice taking care of yourself so that others are okay to the point that you would rather people walk all over you instead of away from you. You put the proverbial oxygen mask on everyone else with disregard for your own need to breathe—until you suffocate.

One of my Austin friends who lives into our city's slogan of "Keep Austin Weird" is a bit too granola to ever put on a varsity jacket, but he will gladly put on his vest while skiing in Vail, Colorado, with the enlightened people. His champion's couture seems far more forward thinking than an antiquated letterman's jacket. The enlightened people notice the vest—and the books, voting practices, and social media posts that go with it. If he wears it long enough and if the enlightened people are generous enough, he will get it—the look of approval that says you are one of us. But it too can make you sweat, because if your identity is based on thinking the right things and checking off every mental box so as to fit in with your designated enlightened group, what happens when there's an issue in which they don't agree with you? If you don't take the party line on every issue, you will find yourself uninvited. The vest prevents you from being honest about your own convictions and how you see the world. But you'd rather sweat in your lie of being "accepted" in their circle than take off the vest and give people the chance to know who you truly are.

While the aesthetic of varsity jacket changes for different people, the Monster of Success will make each and every one of us sweat, because if I am what I do, I'd better find my way into the winner's circle.

7.2 THE PULL
Losing or Loser

PROTECTION

THE PRESENCE OF MONSTERS makes us question our significance.

When you see Jaws swim by your boat,

when you feel Godzilla stomp through your city,

when you hear the huffing and puffing of an asthmatic wolf,

you feel small and insignificant near these terrifying creatures.

The Monster of Success dangles a proverbial carrot in front of us with the promise that attaining success will vanquish the insignificance. It's not completely wrong. Winning helps us gain confidence and identity, especially in adolescence.

It helps a child to discover they can get good grades or they can start a fire better than any other scout in their troop or they can play a wicked bassoon.

When you get a great report card or a merit badge or a . . . um . . . whatever it is you get for playing a bassoon, you stand up taller and look people in the eye a bit easier.*

Success helps keep the fear of insignificance at bay, but no number of trophies or amount of time in the winner's circle completely eradicates the fear. Winning helps you get started in life, but no amount of success makes the fear go away.

JJ Redick, after finishing his college basketball career as the all-time leading scorer in Duke basketball history, was the eleventh overall draft pick in the 2006 NBA draft. At the time of this writing, he's played a dozen years in the NBA and has the fifteenth highest three-point shooting percentage in NBA history. The *New York Times* titled him the "N.B.A.'s Most Meticulous Player" for his year-round obsessive routines and superstitions.[2] His off-season routines include making 342 shots every Sunday. Redick's in-season pregame routine begins twelve hours before tipoff and ranges from eating the same granola bar he's been eating for seven years,† taking the same number of shots, performing the same exercises, and walking back into the locker room at the exact same time before the game. His meticulous preparation and superstitions have earned him a hundred million dollars in salary, yet it hasn't eradicated self-doubt. In a conversation with James Corden about his obsessive routine, Redick said the motivation was fear.[3]

Routines reduce the fear that we are not good enough.

How many of us put in the extra work not simply because of love for our craft but because of the fear of being proven not deserving to be

---

*My friend Jonathan would like you to know two things: there are no merit badges for starting fires and that he holds troop 44's record with 76 merit badges. For more on Jonathan, google "Enneagram 3," and for more on bassoon-ing, check out Rainn Wilson's book *The Bassoon King*.

†It must be a large granola bar.

in the winner's circle? If I believe the lie that I am what I do, there will always be the fear that I am not the parent, the partner, the provider, or the performer that I need to be.

Experimental psychologist Richard Beck writes:

> While we might not fear death on a day-to-day basis, we do fear being a failure in the eyes of others (or ourselves). But failure here is simply a neurotic manifestation of death anxiety, the fear that at the moment of death we won't have accomplished enough to have made a permanent and lasting difference in the world.[4]

The Monster of Success knows our insecurity and fear of nothingness, so it holds out the carrot of success, telling us that if we get the jacket, the corner office, the right position, or the right number of followers, then and only then will we matter. So we get moving. We obsessively ensure that we aren't a failure either now or on the doorstep of eternity because our performance has become shorthand for our identity.

Just think of the language we use to describe failure. When my church informed me that my services would no longer be needed, I never once said, "My performance as a preacher wasn't what it needed to be to keep my job in light of the congregation's financial downturn."

I said, "I got fired."

When your business venture goes under, you don't say that your understanding of the market was wrong.

You say, "I failed."

Our language reveals the substantial pull of the Monster of Success on our self-esteem, because we don't say it's our performance that was unacceptable or our analysis that wasn't successful; we say it was our personhood that failed. We don't differentiate our identity from our performance.

STEAL-ABLE

FOR YEARS, my friend Josh Ross drove an old, greenish Ford Ranger truck. As someone who drives a truck, I don't like to even classify what he drove as a truck. It was more like a station wagon missing the back part of the roof. The truck was put out of its misery after a failed trip back to his home in Memphis from Dallas. The truck stopped running before crossing the Dallas city limits. The mechanic who saw it said the engine was dead, but he generously offered to buy the truck for twenty dollars.

Months before the truck was put out of its and our misery, Josh had a friend riding with him who had been incarcerated for stealing cars. After parking the truck in a rough part of town, Josh asked his friend if he needed to worry about his truck's safety.

To which his friend said,

"Pastor Josh, you don't need to worry about it. Ain't nobody gonna steal your truck."

The devil, the one who steals, kills, and destroys, isn't interested in stealing something with no value.

Laundry trucks don't require bulletproof doors and armed guards.

Only those things that carry the most value will the devil try to steal.

According to the Jewish and Christian traditions, what we do, our work, matters. Therefore, it's likely to be corrupted.

In antiquity, the ruling monarch or king was often seen as the image or likeness of a deity, such as the Egyptian pharaoh King Tut. His actual name is Tutankhamen, which translated means "the living image of Amun." The Egyptian people believed King Tut to be the likeness of Amun, the Egyptian patriarchal deity (think the Egyptian equivalent to the Greek god Zeus).

Unlike their neighbors' creation stories, the Jewish creation story decentralizes power, saying it's not just the king but all people who bear the divine image.

> Then God said, "Let us make humankind in our image, according to our likeness; and let them have dominion over the fish of the sea, and over the birds of the air, and over the cattle, and over all the wild animals of the earth, and over every creeping thing that creeps upon the earth."
>
> > So God created humankind in his image,
> >   in the image of God he created them;
> >   male and female he created them. (Gen. 1:26–27)

Our dominion over creation, that is, our work, displays the divinity within us, meaning work is not a curse that occurs because we are no longer living in paradise. The Greco-Roman culture viewed work as a curse, but work existed before Adam and Eve left the garden of Eden.

Our work reflects the divine calling to exercise dominion over creation as a divine image bearer. By work, I'm not referring to just what you leave home to do each day. Your work is the entirety of what you bring into this world.

It's your paycheck, but it's also your parenting.

It's how you relate to your neighbors and to the earth.

It's how you use your words to build or destroy.

It's the presence and energy you bring into rooms and conversations.

Plato taught that our bodies and our earthly lives don't matter; what really matters is our immortal soul. But that's not the Christian story. Christianity says God created a world that is good, and we have the godlike responsibility to care for this creation. Work mattered before there were nonprofits or church buildings. Work matters because we reflect God and we bring the best out of God's created world. This high calling makes it highly susceptible to being corrupted.

Eugene Peterson writes:

> When we work we are most god-like, which means that it is in our work that it is easiest to develop god-pretensions. Un-sabbathed, our work becomes the entire context in which we define our lives. . . . We lose the capacity to sing "this is my Father's world" and end up chirping little self-centered ditties about what we are doing and feeling.[5]

In its best moments, work reflects our divinity, and in its worst, it reflects our darkness, because we think that what we do is who we are. Work becomes the defining factor of our existence. The pull of the Monster of Success is for you to believe that your work is the entire context by which your life is defined.

And that's why the best thing for us isn't success but failure.

7.3 THE POINT
Not about You

PEP TALK WITH RANDY

A FEW WEEKS AFTER RETURNING from a summer internship in California, I stood at the front of Randy's Monday night preaching class after delivering a fake sermon. Not fake like it didn't exist, but fake like the romance on a reality dating show. It looks real to the eyes, but everyone knows in their hearts that it's just practice.

After a fake sermon in preaching class concludes, classmates give feedback based on an honor code. We all get better grades if everyone honors one another with positive feedback.

I basked in a healthy serving of undeserved honorific compliments, like a seal floating on the ocean basking in sunrays. Randy silently lurked in the shadows, like a great white shark in the depths of the ocean. When I had become fully intoxicated by the compliments and let my defenses down, he attacked.

"Luke, in that story that you told about your female friend, what word did you use to describe her?"

Before I answer that question, I would like to remind the jury that I had returned just a few weeks earlier from a summer spent working with high school students at a church in California, the land of surfer jargon. And like the Bible says, bad company corrupts good morals and judgment on which colloquialisms to use in a fake sermon in preaching class.

"Randy, I . . . uh . . . used the word *chick*."

I assume that a seal can sense when it's in trouble by noticing that all the other seals start to swim away from it. I definitely could sense my impending doom when my classmates leaned away from me when I answered "chick."

Randy covered his face with his hand, forcefully rubbing his thumb into his temple, kind of like when a shark's eyelids* slide over its eyes for protection when it is about to attack its prey.

Randy's hand slid away and his steely gray eyes stared at me.

"Why did you use the word *chick* in a sermon?"

"Um . . . I don't know. I just did."

Then there was silence.

For way too long.

---

*The technical term is *nictitating membrane*.

"So, you used the word *chick* in a sermon because you weren't prepared?"

"Um . . . yes, sir."

And then more pregnant pause until Randy finally said,

"How dare you defame the Word of God by using the word *chick* in a sermon because you weren't prepared!"

"Sorry, sir."

"Don't ever do that again. And class . . . you are all dismissed."

And like a seal so grateful to be alive that it doesn't even care about the bite-size chunk of flesh missing from its abdomen, I slithered out of class.

I must include this fact: Randy called me the next morning at my house to apologize for embarrassing me in front of my friends. An apology that I didn't think he needed to extend that Tuesday morning, and now almost two decades later I'm certain he didn't need to extend. But Randy's the type of person who cares enough to humble himself by asking a dumb twenty-year-old for forgiveness. Which is why I found myself back in front of him, asking for his opinion a year later when I was preparing to be the new speaker at Grace Bible Study.

When you've experienced a Monday-night massacre, you don't have flowery expectations for Randy's counsel, yet somehow he went even darker than I imagined. I wasn't expecting him to tell me that he thought I was great or that he had always expected I'd be leading a large and prominent ministry. But I did not expect the advice he gave.

"Luke, the best thing for you would be to fail."

Have you ever had an overly aggressive, large uncle give you a vicelike-grip hug? The kind of hug in which your face is squeezed against his pearl-snap work shirt and your arms are stuck at your sides until he finally lets you go?

Well, I have.

And that's how I felt when I received that advice.

I lost the ability to breathe.

He kept talking after "the best thing for you would be to fail" but those words were the only ones I could grasp at that moment.

Almost two decades later, I still think that's terrible advice.

It's true.

But terrible.

CHEMO TO THE LIE

I'VE FAILED PLENTY OF TIMES, and it has never felt like the best thing for me.

I've had athletic losses that stung.

I've had professional losses that felt crippling.

And I've had personal losses that have chipped away at my desire to keep going.

Yet I've come to believe that losing can be good for you in the same way that chemotherapy can be good for you.

Losing feels like dying because a death is occurring to the cancerous growth within our hearts that says if we get into the winner's circle, then we will be good enough. Defeat feels like it's killing every last part of us, but when given time to recover, we understand it was only stripping away the deeply intertwined lie that if we win enough, we will be enough.

Sadly, chemo doesn't always work, and neither does failure. Some of us receive chemo but never recover. Some of us experience failure but never realize that our failures (or successes) don't define us. But in the best cases, failure reveals how our identities have become intertwined with the cancerous lie that we are what we do.

At the beginning of Charles Dickens's *A Christmas Carol*, Ebenezer Scrooge sees the spirit of Jacob Marley, his deceased business partner, roaming around restless and shackled with chains. Scrooge can't fathom why his successful business partner should be in such a dispirited state, so he tells him:

> "But you were always a good man of business, Jacob."
>
> "Business!" cried the Ghost, . . . "Mankind was my business. The common welfare was my business; charity, mercy, forbearance, and benevolence were, all, my business. The dealings of my trade were *but a drop of water* in the comprehensive ocean of my business!"[6]

When the Monster of Success has pulled us into believing a drop of water is the comprehensive ocean of our identity, the only way to experience salvation is to drown the lie in the saving waters of defeat.

My friend Bill, a member of Alcoholics Anonymous, shared the following story of another alcoholic.

An alcoholic man got in a car accident while driving drunk, but instead of getting arrested, the cop let him off. The man went home, calling his almost-arrest a miracle, and picked up a bottle of Jack Daniels to celebrate. Two weeks later, he still hadn't stopped the bender—until his body shut down and he died.

Then my friend Bill described his problem:

"He couldn't tell a miracle from a disaster."

The real disaster was that he mistook the officer's leniency for a miracle. If he had gotten a DUI after the accident and gone to jail, he couldn't have drunk himself to death.

The best thing for us isn't always what looks like a miracle.

And the worst thing for us isn't always what looks like a disaster.

Defeat can be the treatment that kills the lie so you can experience the truth. Richard Rohr once told me that success after the age of thirty can't teach you anything.[7] Success gets you going in life, but it can't get you to overcome the lie that you are what you do.

While sitting in Randy's office as a twenty-one-year-old full of excitement and optimism about my opportunity, the jarring nature of the first part of his advice deafened my ears to the rest of it, but after catching my proverbial breath I was able to process his full statement.

"Luke, the best thing for you would be to fail,

because then you would realize that it's not about you."

YOUR CHANCES

EARLY SUCCESS HELPS give us confidence to face the world, but defeat can teach us at any age what has been true all along. It is not, nor has it ever been, as much about us as we think. The lie that I am what I do is buttressed by the secondary lie that what I do is about me. I can believe I am what I do if I also believe I am the master of my own fate.

The American businessman Warren Buffett, who at the time of this writing is the third wealthiest man in the world, hasn't been disillusioned into thinking that his immense professional success is about him. Buffett writes:

> My wealth has come from a combination of living in America, some lucky genes, and compound interest. Both my children and I

won what I call the ovarian lottery. (For starters, the odds against my 1930 birth taking place in the U.S. were at least 30 to 1. My being male and white also removed huge obstacles that a majority of Americans then faced.)

My luck was accentuated by my living in a market system that sometimes produces distorted results, though overall it serves our country well. I've worked in an economy that rewards someone who saves the lives of others on a battlefield with a medal, rewards a great teacher with thank-you notes from parents, but rewards those who can detect the mispricing of securities with sums reaching into the billions.[8]

Leonard Mlodinow, the American theoretical physicist, says it this way:

We're continually nudged in this direction and then that one by random events. As a result, although statistical regularities can be found in social data, the future of particular individuals is impossible to predict, and for our particular achievements, our jobs, our friends, our finances, we all owe more to chance than many people realize.[9]

No matter how much I try to convince myself that my defeats and my successes are solely about me, they aren't. I'm not saying that Warren Buffett's wealth wasn't connected with his talent and work ethic or that Leonard Mlodinow, the son of a survivor of the Holocaust in the Buchenwald concentration camp, stumbled into a doctorate from Berkeley and a *New York Times* #1 bestseller without any personal struggle. But what I think they are both pointing to is that control is an illusion. We might have our hands on the ship's wheel, but we don't control the current, the winds, or what the boats around us do. Here's an example from the church world: How often will Church A celebrate the growth of two hundred members in a year while being willfully ignorant of Church B down the street that finally took a substantial stand against an injustice, resulting in the departure of two hundred of Church B's members—who all just happened to migrate to Church A? Life and our lot within it are far less influenced by our control than many of us want to admit.

WHO ARE YOU?

IN HIS EPONYMOUS JEWISH STORY, Job loses wealth and privilege along with a type of loss that transcends what I'm discussing as the Monster of Success—the loss of his family. In Job 38–41, he cries out to God about the injustice he has experienced and how God has wronged him. In response, God tells him to "gird up [his] loins"[10] and answer several questions:

Were you there when the foundations of the earth were created?

Have you commanded the beginning of the morning?

Have you swum into the sea's springs?

Do you have the ability to call down rain or lightning from the clouds?

Are you the one who makes mighty the horse?

Can you take out the monster Behemoth with hooks?

Can you draw out the monster Leviathan with a fishhook?

After this whirlwind of questioning, Job realizes he doesn't currently nor has he ever had very much understanding or control. Just as we don't.

Our victories are not all our own. They are graces. We participate in them, but we aren't the only ones participating.

The same is true of our defeats.

The Monster of Success says we are nothing if we don't win. And the reason we befriend the Monster of Success is because that is true. We are nothing.

No matter how well we perform, from dust we came and to dust we will return.

No matter how high we climb, we are each still only one of seven billion people.

No matter how much we win, the day we die the world will continue to spin.

The Monster of Success misdiagnoses our nothingness because it acts as though our nothingness can be removed. Our identities will not be found by winning enough.

But it's often in losing that we can be found.

7.4 THE LIGHT
Lose Yourself, Find God

SRR

LET ME TELL YOU about the time I was on TMZ.com.

Technically, all I said was "yeah." Nevertheless, it was a clip of my voice saying an affirmative "yeah" to my guest that week, four-time Olympic gold medalist Sanya Richards-Ross. I frequently get asked which podcast guest I fanboyed about the most. Many assume the answer will be Rainn Wilson, the actor who played Dwight Schrute on *The Office*. As a huge fan of *The Office*, I was very glad that he was a thoughtful and humble person on and off mic, because if he was a jerk it might have ruined my ability to enjoy reruns of *The Office*. But I didn't go full fanboy to the point of taking a picture of myself while sitting in Rainn's car.

However, the first time I went to Sanya's house, I definitely had her take a picture of me wearing her gold medal.

And I might have asked for another picture with another medal of hers the second time I was at her house.

But not the third time because I'm more mature than that. For those Pharisees out there, yes, I did try on her husband's Super Bowl rings that time, but I didn't take any pictures because I am too humble to feel the need to tell everyone about how cool that was.

A month before my "yeah" ended up on TMZ, I received a list of upcoming releases by Zondervan Publishing to see if I'd like to have any of the authors on the podcast. When I saw the name of one of the greatest track athletes ever, I immediately replied because as a track fan how could I not? I ordered her book, and what I read was not what I was expecting. When you've been in the winner's circle as often as Sanya, it would be easy to write only about how you were awesome as a child (Gatorade High School Athlete of the Year), awesome as a young woman (Collegiate National Champ at the University of Texas), and awesome as an adult with a picture-perfect all-American family. But instead, in her book she discussed her greatest loss.

Sanya won a gold medal in the mile relay at the 2004 Olympics, then in 2006 won all six IAAF Golden League events and set the US record in the four-hundred meter.* Sanya entered the 2008 Olympics in Beijing heavily favored to win her first individual gold medal. But the unexpected happened in the four-hundred meter finals: two athletes crossed the finish line before her.

I say she earned a bronze;

she says that she lost.

Everyone was shocked. Even one of the Olympic attendants, in a completely unprofessional move, told Sanya after the race that they had the gold medal ready for her, so how could she lose?

---

*It would also be the world record if not for an East German athlete from 1985 whose record somehow still stands despite substantial doping allegations.

A few hours after the race ended and the medals had been given out, all her teammates went their separate ways. Sanya, finally able to leave the Olympic village, took a city bus to her family's rented apartment for the week. A few stops later, she exited the bus but didn't recognize anything around her. By the time she realized that she'd taken the wrong exit, the bus had already left. She was alone in Beijing, unable to communicate in Mandarin, and unaware of when the next bus would arrive or how she would get to her family.

Sanya, still wearing her red, white, and blue Nike warm-ups, stood lost and alone in Beijing. That was when all the emotions she had been suppressing for weeks flooded over her. It wasn't just the loss of a few hours before but the greatest loss of her life, which had occurred three weeks before, in secret.

Until her book came out, only a few people knew about this loss. As my podcast was the first media to report about the contents of the book, national media like TMZ (along with the *Washington Post* and NBC Sports) referenced my podcast because temporarily it was the only source for the story about Sanya's abortion.

Three weeks before the race, Sanya discovered that she was pregnant. Track is a sport of milliseconds, so even the slight weight gain from that early of a pregnancy would ensure a loss. But Sanya's personal conviction had always been that abortion was wrong. She was forced to choose between her Olympic dream and her personal conviction. She made a decision she regrets to this day and considers the biggest loss of her life.

Three weeks later, after losing the pregnancy and the gold, she stood in Beijing, geographically lost, professionally lost, and personally lost. Yet it was in that moment that all the grief and guilt she had been suppressing to focus on earning a gold medal came to the surface. As Sanya says, it was in that moment of loss that she had the most meaningful spiritual experience of her life. She felt covered by God's grace in a way she had never felt before or since. God met her in her moment of greatest despair.

It wasn't in winning that she found God.

God found her in losing.

FIND GOD IN LOSING

IN *THE MESSAGE*, Eugene Peterson paraphrased Matthew 5:4:

> You're blessed when you feel you've lost what is most dear to you. Only then can you be embraced by the One most dear to you.

At the end of your rope, when you can't hold on anymore,

when you can't pull yourself up any higher,

when you've accepted that you can't find a way back to the top,

a blessing exists because then you can be found by the One who is most dear to you.

This is the story of the prodigal son. It wasn't until he lost all—money, friends, pride—that he finally found the father's love, which had been present the entire time.

When he was living the good life as the son of a wealthy landowner, he missed it.

When he was living a reckless and gluttonous life, he missed it.

It wasn't until he returned home to be a servant at his father's house that he found the love that had always been there for him.

The lie of success is that I've already been found in the winner's circle, so I don't need more. But the chemotherapy-like effect of losing strips away this cancerous lie. When you lose yourself, then you can be found by God.

EMPTY SEATS

THE DOPAMINE-INDUCING "OHHHS" continued, even after I could no longer respond with the "thousand people" answer when asked how many people I preach to. My first job out of school was not a big church, maybe 250 people, but it was in a small town and the church had a nice new building with a big steeple.* When I became that church's preacher, I was a young-looking twenty-four-year-old, so the conversations often went like this:

"You work at that church?"

"Yes, sir."

"Are you the minister for the youths?"

"No, I'm the minister for the everyones."

"Like, the pastor?"

"Yeah. That's me."

"Ohhh wow."

Not exactly the same response, but the you-are-so-young-to-have-that-job "Ohhh wow" still got the dopamine flowing. But a few years later, when I planted a church that never grew to exceed one hundred people, I had to quit the dopamine cold turkey. The response to the how-big-is-your-church question sounded similar—there was only a couple *h*'s difference, but those *h*'s created a massive chasm.

The typical conversation with church-planter Luke went this way:

"What do you do?"

---

*Update: A steeple that since my departure has been destroyed by a hurricane. I'm not saying there is a correlation between me getting fired and the hurricane hitting their building. But I will say that none of the other churches I've worked at that *didn't* fire me when my wife was pregnant ever had a hurricane destroy their steeple.

"I'm a pastor."

"Where is the church?"

"It meets in the wedding chapel by the Harley-Davidson dealership."

"Oh, that's great. How big is it?"

"Just under a hundred people."

"Oh . . . good for you."

It was no longer the "Ohhh" but now it was an "Oh."

Removing those extra *h*'s created a difference. As seen by the typical follow-up line "Oh . . . good for you" or other popular replacement phrases, such as "Oh. That's great" or "Oh. Well, that's nice."

No one needed to use follow-up phrases when the answer was a thousand because no one felt the need to validate me. And they were right; I let the "Ohhh" validate me enough.

The same tricks previously used to steer conversations toward that question now steered them away from it because I didn't feel as though I had started a small church. I felt like I was a failure.

But something changed along the way. I stopped praying for people to attend in order to build an audience to validate me. I stopped praying in a way that commodified people as vehicles to get me into the winner's circle. Instead, I stumbled into this prayer:

"Even if the seats are empty, may my heart be full."

It became a mantra for me.

I said it while driving to church on Sunday mornings.

I said it while unloading the church sound system and children's ministry supplies from our twenty-four-foot trailer.

I said it while going over my notes before the service started.

I even said it while looking over my shoulder during the first song to see who hadn't arrived.

I said it enough times that even I started to believe it.

The church had been around for five years when Lindsay overheard one of our leaders say, "Luke preaches to us the same way he would preach if he were speaking to a thousand people." I'm tearing up as I write these words because that's not where I started. I hadn't always had a heart that was full if the seats were empty, so much so that I used to have the stage lights so bright I couldn't see the empty seats. But over time, the lights could be dimmed and the empty seats didn't deter me because I was being found. My heart was becoming open enough to receive God.

The best thing for you is rarely when you are winning.

The worst thing for you isn't losing.

The presence or absence of success is simply a prop, inviting us to address what resides deep within our souls. The Monster of Success invites us into the mirage of the winner's circle, where the applause drowns out the voice of God. God invites us to lose our lives so that we can be found by the heavenly parent who has always been cheering for us.

SECTION III

A Monster-Friendly Life

To befriend our monsters we must see them, as Parker Palmer says, as "companions to be embraced, guides to be followed, albeit with caution and respect."[1]

When we do, we are like the alcoholic who is grateful for his addiction. Every time he thirsts for more drink, he's trained himself to interpret that longing as a reminder of his need for connection with his Creator.

We are like those who celebrate their failures. Because they point them to finding their identities not in their victories but in the love their Creator has for them.

We are like the religious person who is grateful for her doubts, because they reveal that the Divine isn't reducible to what she can organize into her religious boxes or explanations. And that enables her to rest in her position as the created, not the Creator.

We are like the apostle Paul who said:

> So, I will boast all the more gladly of my weaknesses, so that the power of Christ may dwell in me. Therefore I am content with weaknesses, insults, hardships, persecutions, and calamities for the sake of Christ; for whenever I am weak, then I am strong. (2 Cor. 12:9–10)

Since we've started to develop an appreciation for our monsters as guides that lead us into our Creator's intention for us, it's now time to discuss what a monster-friendly life looks like.

But first, some poetry.

I have a lawyer friend who worked on a case similar to the following story, but since the story is told in the form of a poem, no one should get sued for discussing confidential information.

> There once was a celebrity who liked to punch out,
> who had an employee who enjoyed a lunch out.
> While eating barbecue a lovely woman he met,
> to impress, he invites her to see his boss's tiger pet.
> Without washing her hands she thinks it's neat,
> the tiger did too, thinking she smelled like a treat.
> Into the cage her arm went for a little cuddle,
> then to the ground her arm dropped into a bloody puddle.

The life lesson is this: when living with a monster, you are required to do certain things, like not smell like barbecue when you pet it.

For starters, living a monster-friendly life requires honesty. As Psalm 36:1–2 says:

> Transgression speaks to the wicked
>   deep in their hearts;
> there is no fear of God
>   before their eyes.
> For they flatter themselves in their own eyes
>   that their iniquity cannot be found out and hated.

As long as we deceive ourselves, we will never befriend what resides deep within our hearts. A monster-friendly life doesn't happen without clean hands and an honest heart, which speak to the overarching point. A monster-friendly life requires intentionality. As the old adage goes, failing to plan is planning to fail. If one doesn't take seriously one's own spiritual wellness, the state of one's soul can go sideways very quickly. The last section of this book gives you three principles for intentionally living a monster-friendly life:

How (not) to dress for your monster.

Where (not) to find your monster.

What (not) to expect about your monster.

These three principles can help you live into the life your Creator intends for you while also preventing your arm from getting ripped off.*

---

*Technically speaking, I can't promise that.

8

How (Not) to Dress
for Your Monster

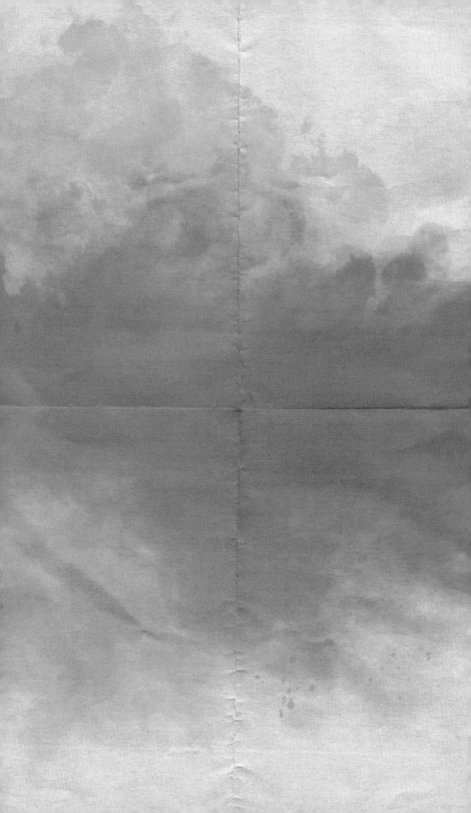

Chubs

ONCE UPON A TIME in a land far, far away, little Frankie strolled down to the pond where alone he stood in the predawn darkness, waiting for his dad to join him at their normal spot to watch the sun break over their farm. Frankie arrived before his father's required coffee had finished brewing, yet Frankie wasn't alone. A pair of eyes met him in the darkness on the other side of the pond. Frankie didn't have too many years, but he had enough to be familiar with most creatures on the farm—but not this one. Frankie couldn't place the species, but whatever it was, he was looking directly into its eyes. Its gangly feet were too big for its legs. A thick tail brushed the ground. Its squared head with the foreshadowing of horns hung low, overmatching its undersized neck.

Frankie's feet didn't move as he was unsure if the creature was friend or foe, but his heart had already decided that this awkward juvenile animal was to be his pet. Frankie knew his father did not want any more animals on the farm, but that was a problem to be solved later. The problem at hand was to convince this animal to be friendly.

Frankie tiptoed around the pond through mud and overgrown grass. Nearing the creature, he extended his right arm, fingers clasped together in a fist so as to save his fingers in case the creature snapped at him.

"Boy, I sure hope you are nice," he said.

The heavy head drooped lower.

Frankie slowly placed his hand behind its ear, extended his fingers, and began petting. The thick tail began to sway.

Frankie's new friend followed him back to the farm, where Frankie hid him among the other animals. Within a few months, this creature grew from the size of a svelte Great Dane to the size of a husky thoroughbred, earning him the name "Chubs."

One day, Frankie went out to the field to plow with Chubs at his side. Frankie tried to coax a reluctant ox into putting on the yoke but with no success. Chubs, seeing his owner's plight, nudged his way between the ox and Frankie, putting his head under the yoke. Frankie gave Chubs his chance, a decision that quickly seemed brilliant as Chubs pulled the plow twice as fast as even his most enthusiastic oxen. The oxen got Wally Pipped.*

From that day on, Frankie's work was done more quickly and efficiently. Frankie's surprised father gave him more praise and more responsibility, even taking out another mortgage to buy more land for his suddenly skilled son to oversee.

Frankie's dad saw the extra crops, but he didn't see the downside. The unworked oxen went soft, and the horses grew weak as Chubs pirated their food. Chubs stood two heads taller than all the animals, which were now homeless because Chubs had taken over the entire barn. Chubs still got the work done, but now it was on his own terms. Chubs knew he was the one getting everything done, and he knew Frankie needed him. Over time, he morphed from the one that helped Frankie into the one that haunted Frankie.

Frankie knew Chubs couldn't stay any longer. But how could he get rid of him after Chubs had gotten him this far?

---

*For all you non-baseball fans, that's a reference to the guy who missed one game and was replaced by Lou Gehrig, who played the next 2,130 games consecutively and became arguably the best first baseman ever. I know I could have just said he lost his job, but then you still wouldn't know who Wally Pipp was.

Frankie learned the hard way that just because something gets the job done doesn't mean it's good for you.

I once read a comment that went something like this: evil crosses our doors first as a stranger, then becomes a friend, but doesn't leave until it has become our master. The stranger initially seems like a heaven-sent gift, but given enough time it creates a hell for us. The most destructive monsters are the ones that, at first glance, don't appear to be monsters at all.

Man of War

He had always imagined his journey would lead him to battle, but today he carried no swords, only sandwiches. The days in the field tending the sheep had taught him to fight off animals with a slingshot and boredom with fantasies of being a mighty warrior. Today's daydream felt real, because the road he walked on ended at an actual battlefield where the sandwiches' recipients, his brothers, were stationed. The same brothers who thought all his battles were only daydreams, despite having seen the carcasses of the defeated lion and bear.

Today's daydream concluded as the battleground appeared. Lost among the masses and unable to see his brothers, he began to yell,

"Eliab!

Abinadab!

Shammah!"

His mouth opened again to repeat the names, but his ears heard another voice over his own. He closed his mouth to process what had occurred, when the voice thundered again. This time he understood the words:

"Choose a man for yourselves, and let him come down to fight me!"

A stampede ensued as soldiers shed their weapons and ran homeward. His own brothers ran past him without so much as an acknowledgment.

He didn't follow.

He had to see the source of the voice.

What he saw was a man larger than a bear, standing on legs like tree trunks wrapped in bronze, wearing a coat of chainmail that must have weighed as much as he himself weighed. A javelin hung across his back, and a spear the diameter of a horse's leg was in his hand. The sight of this monster mesmerized him.

A hand grabbed his shoulder and turned him around.

"David, you have no place here. Go home before you get yourself killed and get us in trouble," said his oldest brother, Eliab.

Angered equally by his brother's doubt and the giant's disrespect, he turned back to the battleground where he found his people's own giant. King Saul, who on better days stood head and shoulders above every man in Israel, today was slumped over, enabling a teenage boy to get his attention.

"My King, I have faced monsters in the field before. What could this giant do to me that a lion or a bear couldn't do?"

Eliab's eyes rolled.

Saul shook his head, lifted his hands, and with a resigned sigh said,

"Why not, kid?"

Saul didn't have anyone else willing to fight, so he thought why not let this boy get killed so we can get on with becoming enslaved by Goliath and his people. Like rearranging furniture on the *Titanic*, Saul decided to make this boy at least look like a man of war. He placed on the boy his own bronze helmet and coat of chainmail. Then Saul handed him his sword.

The once fleet-of-foot David could now not even lift a toe.

Armor

FRIEDRICH NIETZSCHE SAID, "He who fights with monsters should look to it that he himself does not become a monster.. And when you gaze long into an abyss, the abyss also gazes into you."[1]

When standing toe-to-toe with your fears, it's natural to clothe yourself with protection without regard for the long-term effects, like David being clothed with Saul's armor after gazing into the eyes of Goliath. In the beginning, after Adam and Eve had their naiveté and nudity revealed to them by eating the forbidden fruit, they clothed themselves with fig leaves. And today we clothe ourselves with the vast array of armor at our disposal:

Approval, because if others like me, I must not be insignificant.

Power, because if I get strong enough, nothing can hurt me.

Pleasure, because if I can feel comfortable enough, I will not feel the pain.

Control, because if I have control, I won't seem weak and small.

Mastery, because if I can make it good enough, I will feel good about myself and the voice inside my head will become quiet.

The Austrian psychotherapist who coined the phrase "inferiority complex," Alfred Adler, says we armor ourselves with these types of behavior to overcome feelings of inferiority.[2] These pursuits don't necessarily seem destructive. Approval doesn't seem bad because we were created for connection and community. Power doesn't seem bad as we were created with a call to exercise dominion over the earth. Pleasure doesn't seem bad since we were gifted a world with comforts. They don't seem bad, but neither did it seem bad for David to put on Saul's armor or for little Frankie to bring home Chubs.

The Giant

In 1946, ANDRÉ RENÉ ROUSSIMOFF was born in the foothills of the French Alps in the town of Grenoble. By the age of seventeen, he overshadowed his four siblings, standing six feet, seven inches tall. A French-Canadian professional wrestler saw André and brought him to North America to wrestle, where André found his life's work. By the age of twenty-six, his notoriety and his stature had grown exponentially. He had wrestled in front of twenty thousand fans, stood over seven feet tall, and weighed over five hundred pounds. That year the world's largest wrestling promotion, World Wide Wrestling Federation (now known as the WWE), signed him and gave him the name André the Giant. In 1987, a record-setting ninety-three thousand fans packed Detroit's Pontiac Silverdome for WrestlingMania III to watch André the Giant wrestle Hulk Hogan.

His size, along with his ample charisma, turned André René Roussimoff into a superstar with the moniker "The Eighth Wonder of the World," but it also killed him. André the Giant had acromegaly, a condition that filled his body with an abundance of growth hormones and ultimately caused him to die from congestive heart failure alone in a Paris hotel at the age of forty-six. Doctors had offered him medical treatment to combat the effects of acromegaly, but André had refused because he thought the treatment would impede his wrestling.

In a culture that obsesses over production and results, we rarely stop to wonder about the long-term effects of what is helping us get through the day. We are like Frankie and his monster Chubs; we can't get rid of what has brought us so far, no matter how much pain it brings us. We don't consider shedding the armor, regardless of its negative effects, because we don't trust that our authentic and unencumbered self can stand on its own.

But, like David, for you to have a chance to succeed, you've got to shed the armor.

False Self

WHAT I AM CALLING ARMOR is what Thomas Merton called the false self. Defining Merton's term, Richard Rohr says, "The False Self is who you think you are. Your thinking does not make it true. Your False Self is almost entirely a social construct to get you started on your life journey."[3]

To explain the false self, let me do what my psychologist father would frown upon: some armchair psychoanalysis of a biblical character, the rich young ruler.

In Mark's Gospel, the rich young ruler approaches Jesus to ask him what he must do to inherit eternal life. Jesus tells him to keep all the commandments. The rich young ruler proudly responds that he's kept all the commandments since he was a boy. Then Jesus says the words that leave the rich young ruler crestfallen. Jesus tells him to sell everything and give the money to the poor.

The rich young ruler looked successful to everyone who saw him, yet underneath his armor of good religious performance, the darkness in his soul—his fear-driven obsession with money—had never experienced the light. His false self got him going in life. It got him to obey all the commandments, but it didn't give him peace. Otherwise, why would he feel the need to create what looks like some community theater in which Jesus is a prop in his attempt to tell everyone (and himself) how well he's lived his life? If the interaction wasn't performance, he would have at least been somewhat willing to change when Jesus answered his question. But Jesus was probably just the latest rabbi to enter his town from whom to gain the approval he craved. As a Jewish child growing up in a tumultuous time, when the Jews lived under Roman oppression, the rich young ruler probably believed his acts of piety would help bring about the redemption of Israel. His good performance brought approval from religious leaders like the Pharisees, who shared a similar view about holiness leading to Israel's redemption. His obedience protected him from feeling inferior, but it never enabled him to access the dark recesses of his soul.

The false self continues to earn degrees, high-level jobs, and no small amount of respect. But just as the best bank robbery is the one that no one ever knows happened, the most pernicious monster is the one that hacks into your identity without you ever knowing it exists.

Your false self is just that monster.

The English word *personality* is derived from the Greek word *prosopon* that means "mask." Our personality isn't our truest self; it's the mask we've put on to get started in life. We don't ask if it can have a monstrous effect on us. David put on Saul's armor because it made sense to wear armor when he was about to face an armor-clad giant. We put on a personality early in life to navigate a big, scary world.

Our false self or our personality is often what pleases authority figures, whether they are parents, teachers, or our ideal peer group. Some of us have learned how to obediently follow all the rules and become trustworthy team players so that people will appreciate us and give us authority.

Others have learned how to charm people by making a well-timed joke or cracking a tension-breaking smile, which makes people gravitate toward them while overlooking their transgressions.

Others have learned how to make people feel valued by helping them so they will in turn be liked.

People like these parts of our personalities, but that doesn't mean they actually like us—because we aren't our personalities or our masks or our armor or our false selves.

Many liked the personality of the rich young ruler. Many wanted their daughters to marry him and their sons to be his friend. But I'd wager no one actually loved him except the only person who saw past his performance and saw him—Jesus.

"Jesus, looking at him, loved him and said, 'You lack one thing; go, sell what you own.'"[4]

Many before had looked at his personality and liked his personality, but Jesus looked beyond his false self and loved him.

Religious people's armor can be challenging to detect because churches love rule followers, gifted people, charming people, and those willing to help. Churches will polish your armor and tell everyone about your great armor. Just as people did with the rich young ruler. But Jesus looked past his armor to love him, and Jesus looks past yours to love you.

Temporary Armor

CARL STOOD ON THE DOCK with a smile that only a fishing trip with Dad can put on a ten-year-old boy's face. As Carl cast his rod, his sandals slipped on the dock. He reached for a rail to keep from falling into the water. As his hand grasped the rail, he dropped his fishing pole. Carl's beloved fishing rod bounced off the dock, under the railing, and down into the water. Before the rod sank completely out of sight, he felt his father's hands grab the back of his T-shirt, lift him off the ground, and toss him against the rail.

"Stupid Carl," his dad said.

At that moment, something changed within Carl.

From then on, Carl didn't get sad when his dad wasn't around, because if his dad wasn't around, Carl and his mom couldn't be abused by him. At the age of ten, Carl knew that he didn't ever want to be like his father. He didn't want to treat his children like his dad treated him. He didn't want to talk like him or even think like him. Every decision was based on not being his father.

Carl's father didn't spend time with his kids, so Carl was the parent who volunteered at school and was the coach for all his daughters' softball teams.

Carl's father wasn't religious, so Carl became a pastor.

Carl's entire existence was based on not being his father. And this worked well for Carl. It built him a great family, wonderful kids, and a successful career.

Until his father found God.

Like Saul of Tarsus on the road to Damascus, Carl's dad saw the light and made a one-hundred-eighty-degree change. He saw the errors of his former ways and created a new path, extending apologies and developing a profound interest in his grandkids' lives. Which was a positive change for everyone except Carl, because Carl's existence was now based on not being someone who no longer existed.

Carl's armor, the I'm-not-going-to-be-him armor, didn't fit anymore.

Just as Jesus did with the rich young ruler, Jesus sees the true Carl and invites him to go deeper. Just as Jesus invites all of us to go deeper.

Jesus sees our armor yet loves us. Jesus calls us to go past the performances and the personality to experience the truest version of ourselves.

Truth and Death

LONG BEFORE THE STORY of Victor Frankenstein's homemade monster was written, twenty versions of the legend of Golem of Prague existed. In one iteration of the story of Golem, Judah Loew, a sixteenth-century rabbi, creates out of clay an innocent but bumbling giant to protect the Jews from the then regular anti-Semitic attacks in the Jewish ghetto of Prague. Rabbi Loew brought the giant clay sculpture to life by writing the Hebrew word for truth, *emet*, on Golem's forehead.

Rabbi Loew made him strong and powerful to be a capable defender, but Golem followed directions either too literally or incorrectly. Golem protected the Jews, but his clumsy and dumb nature also accidentally harmed them, forcing Rabbi Loew to shut down the bumbling giant. To put Golem of Prague out of commission, Rabbi Loew erased the first *e* from his forehead, changing the word from *truth* to *death*.[5]

We've all created our own homemade defense systems, our own armor, and the only way to prevent further harm is by putting to death our false self with truth.

We must put to death

the lie that we are what pleases other people,

the lie that our identity is tied to how others feel about us,

the lie that our good behavior makes us good,

the lie that only happiness makes the moment meaningful.

David had to get rid of his armor too. David tried on the armor of the Israelite giant, Saul, as he prepared to face the Philistine giant, Goliath, but it made him immobile. David was about to battle a monster, and Saul made the all-too-natural decision to make him look like a monster. David was an inexperienced soldier, which is why he didn't have his own armor, but David was seasoned with bravery and quickness. Saul, who did not understand David's strengths, attempted to lessen David's obvious physical weaknesses. But by doing so, he unknowingly also disarmed David's only shot at victory.

Being a mediocre version of Goliath meant that David could never be the best version of himself. David ultimately shed the armor so that he could be who he was uniquely gifted to be.

Our false self pretends to be our truth and the way to defend ourselves against our monsters.

But we must put aside these false truths to be who we were created to be. Just as Paul says in Galatians 2:20, "My old self has been crucified with Christ. It is no longer I who live, but Christ lives in me" (NLT).

Paul's old self wasn't bad. We might think the killing of people in other religions, as Saul did, was bad. But in the Jewish mind, he was being zealous for righteousness, as had many Jewish leaders before him.[6] As Paul said to the church at Philippi, it was only considered bad because of what it competed against:

> If someone else thinks they have reasons to put confidence in the flesh, I have more: circumcised on the eighth day, of the people of Israel, of the tribe of Benjamin, a Hebrew of Hebrews; in regard to the law, a Pharisee; as for zeal, persecuting the church; as for righteousness based on the law, faultless.

> But whatever were gains to me I now consider loss for the sake of Christ. What is more, I consider everything a loss because of the surpassing worth of knowing Christ Jesus my Lord, for whose sake I have lost all things. I consider them garbage. (Phil. 3:4–8 NIV, emphasis added)

He considers his former self as garbage, not because it was inherently bad but because of the surpassing value of knowing Christ. To know

Christ, the One who is the fullest and clearest picture of what humanity was intended to be, is how we know our truest self.

Your armor, like Paul's, may not be categorically bad. You may be like David and need to remove noble armor. It's noble to try to please people or to bring laughter into every room or to make things efficient and productive, but it cannot compare to your truest self.

Star

THE FIRST TIME I WENT to a therapist was an awkward experience because my therapist wanted to talk about feelings. We had the following dialogue:

"Luke, I hear you talking about what concerns you intellectually. But I don't hear you discussing your feelings."

"Um . . . thank you?"

"No, Luke, I think you should try dealing with your feelings more."

"That's an interesting idea; I will think about it."

I actually said I will *think* about *feeling* more.

Luckily, he didn't refer me to another therapist at that point, because he later recommended a book that finally gave me the language to understand what I now recognize as part of my false self.

He recommended the book *Adult Children of Alcoholics*, a peculiar recommendation since my parents aren't alcoholics. We never even had alcohol in the house, except for the time when I was nine and my mom made beer-battered shrimp. Here's some advice to any nine-year-olds reading this that I wish someone had given me when I was your age: you can't get drunk from eating beer-battered shrimp, so no need to stumble around the house while slurring your words and declaring that the shrimp made you feel "really woozy."

I didn't think a book about alcoholic parents was a good fit for someone who grew up in a teetotaler home until he explained the commonalities of adult children of alcoholics and adult children of parents with chronic illness. Alcoholic parents often create chaotic systems in which everything revolves around their dysfunction. Family members compensate so the family can stay afloat, despite Dad drinking up the month's rent again or Mom again missing an event because she is passed out. The family learns how to keep the ship sailing in spite of one member's sabotage.

A parent with a chronic illness, like my mom, can cause a similar dynamic because everyone caters to the limitation created by the illness. Mom can't travel. Mom needs to rest. Mom can't make lunches for school. It's the same game of keeping the ship afloat around the illness.

Let me be clear, it is not totally fair to equate the dynamics created by alcoholism and chronic illness for many reasons, but the book's argument is that the long-term effect on children can look similar.

The typical four roles played by adult children of alcoholics are the placater (who fixes everything), the scapegoat (or family problem), the adjuster, and the hero/star child.[7]

I'd like to think that high school–age Luke didn't curse or drink but did read his Bible every day simply because of his commitment to Jesus, but we are all a mixed bag of motivations. I'd like to think I became a preacher simply because of the beauty of Jesus, but the human heart is a mystery. Simplistic answers about motivation don't suffice.

Somewhere along the way, I started to believe that I mattered because I was more religious than my peers. The star-child role helped me never get a DUI. It helped me get into college when I was sixteen. It helped me read my Bible every day. But it came at a price. Like David languishing under Saul's armor, I was trying to be someone I wasn't.

When you feel you have to be better than everyone else, what do you do when you come to grips with the fact that your own humanity is not any different from those around you?

What do you do when you see yourself as the person who helps others, but then realize the people you are trying to help have just as much divinity within them as you do? What do you do when you realize you need to take just as many notes as you are giving?

When you realize there's only one star of the show and it's not you, it makes you wonder who you really are.

My false self helped me as a nineteen-year-old to get up every Sunday morning to drive forty-five minutes to preach at rural churches. It prevented me from getting into trouble in the party scene. It did some good things for me, but it wasn't the best that God had for me.

As I've begun naming my armor, I haven't discarded my religious practices or my calling, but I do approach them differently now because I realize that my truest self isn't my best performance any more than it is my worst performance.

Remember

IN THE BEGINNING, humanity was created, both male and female, in the image of God. Not just royalty—everyone. When humanity left the garden, God did not make us leave our divinity. That same divinity still exists within us, underneath the armor that we wear and behind the distorted self that the dark pull has contorted us into being. This divinity must be unearthed, so we can remember who God truly created us to be.

Our truest self is remembered, not created.

The ancient Greek Stoics taught that God placed a soul into a body only when a baby was already fully formed in its mother's womb.

Immediately after putting the soul into the body, God would seal off the memory of its preexistence by physically shutting the baby's lips with God's finger, so the baby would never speak about it. Yet somewhere deep within our subconscious, we faintly remember. The Stoics say we have a little cleft under our noses, just above the center of our lips, because that's where God's finger sealed our lips. Maybe that's why, when we seek to remember something, we place a finger in the little cleft under our nose. We are trying to access a memory buried deep within us. We are remembering, not creating.

Fr. Ronald Rolheiser says, "In this life, we don't learn truth, we recognize it; we don't learn love, we recognize it; and we don't learn what is good, we recognize it. We recognize these qualities because we already possess them in the core of our souls."[8]

This is the endgame of spiritual formation: living into who God intended us to be. Yet we can't arrive there on our own. Enneagram master teacher and friend Suzanne Stabile says we can't get rid of personality because the way we would go about getting rid of our personality would be through our personality. We would try to achieve it or charm it or perfect it into happening, and that doesn't work. Instead, we must allow personality to fall away through the work of God.

It's a work of God.

This soul work will lead you away from your comforts and into your fears. It will be painful and disorienting as it strips away what you know and what has served you well. But follow where God leads you because you can trust that the same power that raised Jesus from the dead is at work in you, resurrecting you to become whole and complete.

When invited to remove your armor by going into the dark, go, but not because you think it will be easy or painless. Go because your truest self is underneath, waiting to be found. A monster-friendly life is not one dressed in your false self; it's one that's committed to living out of your truest self.

9

Where (Not) to Find Your Monster

You're in Grad School?

AT THIS POINT IN THE BOOK, you might still be wondering, *What exactly is my monster?*

Sadly, I can't answer that question, but I can point you to where you need to go for the answer. It's the place my friend and experimental psychologist Richard Beck calls the epistemic limits.

I know this term probably doesn't help much because most of us don't talk like experimental psychologists. More on that later, but first let me tell you another story.

I sat in the second row next to my good friend Josh Ross on day three of a weeklong graduate course. To spice up the eight hours of lecturing I would be listening to, I brought one of the nicest gifts my wife has ever given me: *Air Jaws II*. Nothing says love like a documentary about the feeding patterns of great white sharks, specifically the white shark's tendency to jump out of* the water to attack seals.

With our noon lunch break an hour away, I clandestinely insert the DVD into my Dell laptop, thinking the documentary will make for nice premeal entertainment. Mark the Pacifist sits in the row behind us unaware of the ensuing in-class entertainment, much like the seals in the documentary. Within seconds, an audible groan emerges from Mark the Pacifist as my screen displays a fifteen-foot shark flying out of the ocean with half of a seal carcass in its mouth. A not-so-gentle elbow from Ross informs me that our suspicious professor is now hunting me.

---

*The technical term is *breach*.

I lean forward to shut my laptop and to evade the professor.

As I extend my body forward, I sneeze.

A normal sneeze, like I've done thousands of times, but what follows has never happened before or since.

The left side of my face goes numb, and like rain cascading off the gentle pitch of a roof, the numbness slowly spills down my left arm into my left hand.

Next, a headache grows. Not the I'm-a-little-tired-or-dehydrated kind of headache but the Why-did-someone-strike-my-head-with-a-mallet? type.

I return an elbow to Ross and he says, "Not yet."

"Not the DVD, Ross," I whisper. "Something is wrong with me."

Ross, who clearly hasn't taken any pastoral care classes yet, says, "Sorry, man."

I'm not sure what response I was looking for, but my half-numb face and fully numb left arm make me think I'm becoming Harvey "Two-Face" Dent; so I think I merit more than a "sorry, man."

So alone I sit, unnerved.

Or to be more specific, half unnerved.

I plan to wait out this issue until our noon lunch break, because I don't want to be rude and leave the class early. For the record, yes, my twenty-three-year-old self would be rude enough to watch a shark documentary in class. But no, not rude enough to interrupt the professor by leaving class early.

I'm halfway to noon when my numbness and headache are joined by nausea, forcing a change in my departure time.

"Ross, I'm not feeling good. I've got to go."

And again, I receive another nonplussed response from my fellow Bible student Ross, who apparently hasn't been introduced to the passage in the Bible about bearing one another's burdens. I pack up my bag and walk out of class. At least Mark the Pacifist seems downtrodden that I am leaving, though it might have been because the PETA agents he has called haven't yet arrived to arrest me.

I hope to receive medical care from my nurse wife at home but find our house's only occupants are our two dogs. Neither of them offer much medical help.

I am now forced to call upon Mr. Compassion, Josh Ross, to ask him to pick me up and drive me to the hospital.

In his defense, he did take me, even after I walked out to his green Ford Ranger with a trash can in hand. In my defense, if I had vomited on the truck, it wouldn't have hurt the truck's value.

Upon arriving at the hospital, I'm quickly escorted to a room. Lindsay comes down from the maternity floor to join us. The emergency room doctor arrives and asks for the story. So I tell him about sitting in my graduate class, the sneeze, then the numb face, left arm, left hand, and then the headache and vomiting.

The way he shakes his head lets me know that's not enough detail for him.

I begin telling him about *Air Jaws II* when he interrupts—

"Luke, did you have any headaches before today?"

"No."

"Any blurry vision?"

"No."

"Stiff neck?"

"Yes, doctor, I actually do have a stiff neck."

"How long has your neck been stiff?"

"Since Monday."

"What was Monday?"

Monday is, as any weight lifter knows, chest day.

The doctor asks if I did anything different on chest day.

Which brings up a new story with a similar cast of characters.

After finishing class Monday afternoon, Ross and I went into the university's field house where I ran into an old meathead gym friend who had a new exercise that he described as a push-up on steroids.

So, of course, I was going to try it.

On the opposite side of the gym, two gymnastics rings hung in a squat rack two feet off the ground, parallel to a bar a body's length away that is also suspended two feet off the ground. I leaned down and put my hands into the rings and then placed my feet on the bar. Now I was in a push-up position, hovering two feet above the ground. Next, the meathead friend placed on my head a leather weight-lifting belt that was attached by a chain to a seventy-two-pound kettlebell.

I'm now challenged to try ten push-ups from the suspended position with the seventy-two-pound kettlebell hanging from my head.

It's not essential to the story to say I did the ten weighted push-ups.

It definitely doesn't add anything to the story to say I did those ten weighted push-ups quite easily.

But in case you were wondering, that is exactly what happened.

After the workout, I didn't think twice about my herculean display of strength and stupidity.

Tuesday morning, I woke up with a little crick in my neck.

By Shark Day, there was substantial soreness.

I finish the story, and the doctor is silent for a few seconds and then says,

"You thought it was a good idea to hang a seventy-pound weight from your head," and then, turning to Lindsay, "and your husband said that he was in graduate school?"

I raise my non-numb arm. "Technically speaking, doctor, it was not seventy pounds. It was seventy-two pounds."

The doctor then began treating the reason for my trip to the ER, but it wasn't what I was expecting. The doctor didn't treat my vomiting with an antinausea medicine. He didn't examine the numb skin on my face or arm. His assault on my brain activity notwithstanding, he didn't look at my head where my headache resided.

He sent me for an x-ray on my neck.

The issue wasn't where I felt the symptoms—my face, arm, hand, head, or stomach. The location of the issue was much deeper. If he had just dealt with the symptoms, he would never have found the root of the issue: the disk in my neck that temporarily slipped out of place when I sneezed.

Symptoms are easier to identify, but putting Band-Aids on symptoms doesn't solve the root issue. It would be like when my daughter said she had a skeedy monster on the ceiling of her room. I could have gotten rid of the red light by placing masking tape over it, but that would have also masked the warning the light was intended to be. Masking the symptoms doesn't get you where you need to be for salvation.

But your epistemic limits do.

Running

IMAGINE YOU ARE OUT for an early morning run through your neighborhood. You've run it so many times that you could do it with your eyes closed. You leave your driveway the same time of day, make the same left-hand turn at the elementary school down the hill, touch the same light post a mile later, then turn around to take the same path home. When your house becomes visible again, the school bell rings as always.

But this morning, just as you touch the light post, you stumble upon an unwanted guest—a massive German shepherd coming straight for you with no leash-carrying owner chasing after him. No ladder or tree invites you to climb up to safety.

What happens next?

Your fight-or-flight response kicks in, adrenaline rushes through your veins, and you sprint home like Usain Bolt. You get away from the dog, and before you know it you are home, sitting down, shoes off, with a drink in your hand when you hear the school bell ring.

Because nothing gets us running like fear.

Monsters and the fears they represent motivate us to move. They sure did for George. But too often we run in the direction of symptoms, not solutions.

George was a troubled but successful thirty-year-old salesman with an acceptable marriage and a painful childhood. While on a business trip, George and his wife visited a cathedral in Montreal where he put fifty-five cents in an offering box. As George dropped the coins into the box, a thought shot through his mind:

You are going to die at the age of fifty-five.

Two weeks later, that random thought removed a decade of life expectancy as it now said he was going to die at the age of forty-five. The ominous thoughts continued, becoming more detailed and haunting. He was going to be murdered or a collapsed roof would kill him or a bridge or an excavation site.

George tried to overcome these disturbing thoughts by confronting them. He drove to the bridge on which he imagined dying and then to the excavation site. The plan worked to eradicate the thoughts. George would get out of bed when a haunting thought popped up and drive to the ominous location at all hours of the night. With his fearful thought conquered, he returned home to sleep for what was left of the night. The cycle continued the next day: bad thought, drive to location, return home. Soon George was driving every night while getting less and less sleep. Which led him into psychiatrist Scott Peck's office and three months of unsuccessful counseling.

As Peck tells it in his book *People of the Lie*, the story peaked during a conversation in his office when a seemingly refreshed and rejuvenated George told Peck that he was better now because he had made a deal with the devil (including his son Christopher in the bargain) that caused the thoughts to cease.

As a general rule of thumb, when you tell your psychiatrist about your Faustian deal, the conversation gets quite interesting. Peck, after the obligatory dramatic pause, looked at George and dropped the unbridled truth:

> "Basically, George, you're kind of a coward," I continued. "Whenever the going gets a little bit rough, you sell out. When you're faced with the realization that you're going to die one of these days, you run away from it. You don't think about it, because it's 'morbid.' When you're faced with the painful realization that your marriage is lousy, you run away from that too. Instead of facing it and doing something about it, you don't think about that either. And then because you've run away from these things that are really inescapable, they come to haunt you in the form of your symptoms, your obsessions and compulsions. These symptoms could be your

salvation. You could say, 'These symptoms mean that I'm haunted. I better find out what these ghosts are, and clean them out of my house.' But you don't say that, because that would mean really facing some things that are painful. So you try to run away from your symptoms too. Instead of facing them and what they mean, you try to get rid of them. And when they're not so easy to get rid of, you go running to anything that will give you relief, no matter how wicked or evil or destructive."[1]

Fear gets you moving, but rarely does it get you moving in the direction of the real issue. It was easier for George to drive to a bridge or an excavation site than to address his childhood trauma or his unhappy marriage. Just like it was easier for Jonah to embark on a futile attempt to flee God than to confront the hatred within his heart.

Fear gets us moving, but often it's moving in the direction of the symptoms and not the source. Fear makes us look at the destruction on the surface but ignore the subterranean monsters creating the destruction.

It's easier to know the effect of the monster on the surface than the monsters residing in the darkest cave, on the highest mountain, in the deepest part of the sea, behind the curtains, or in the closet. Richard Beck describes these places as the epistemic limits because they exist at the limits of knowing. If you want to know your monster, you must venture beyond your current limits.

Shallow Emotion

WHEN I WAS YOUNGER, I never feared death, but whatever it was that prevented my fear of death disappeared when I became a father.

Upon the birth of my first daughter, I unintentionally started a countdown for how long until she could survive on her own without me.

When I have a speaking gig, I want to know exactly how long they expect me to preach. It's kind of like that but just a bit darker.

I initially assumed her turning eighteen to be the checkpoint, after which I would be free to do whatever dangerous endeavor I wanted: skydiving, riding a motorcycle, talking politics in elders' meetings. But then I thought of her navigating college, career choices, and marriage without a father, and the number got bumped back even further. The ensuing appearance of her two younger sisters has since reset the countdown twice. Needless to say, I'll be taking my vitamins for a while.

I've tried to get to the source of this fear, and I'm starting to think it's not death I actually fear.

I fear my daughters not having their dad.

Maybe that's why I admire the Rev. Becca Stevens so much. She's created a great life. She has a family, kids, and a meaningful career as the founder of an amazing organization, Thistle Farms, even though she experienced my nightmare. When Becca was five, her father, who was also a pastor, died in a car accident.

In the aftermath of the tragedy, a new pastor, under the guise of helping the grieving family, became close enough that he could abuse little Becca over multiple years.

An unconscionable transgression.

The story of a pastor abusing the child of a deceased pastor fills me with anger no matter how many times I hear it, yet I've never heard Becca sound angry when telling the story. So I finally asked her why she didn't seem angry.

To which she responded,

"Anger is a shallow emotion."[2]

Against my wishes, that quote stuck with me for weeks. In moments of quiet, the phrase tiptoed into my headspace. In moments when daydreaming about the singular comment I could have and should have said to win a tense conversation the day before, Becca's quote stomped through my psyche.

Until I accepted the reverend's wisdom that anger is a shallow emotion.

We've all seen this in action in the road-rage guy. While driving home from work, he acts like he wants to fight the driver who cut him off, but his rage isn't actually about the other driver. His rage comes from the deeper and unaccessed emotions caused by his demeaning boss at work or the emasculating criticism from his wife waiting for him at home. It's easier for him to yell at the back of a car than to confront the feelings of inadequacy and insufficiency.

James Baldwin, the American novelist, said, "I imagine one of the reasons people cling to their hate so stubbornly is because they sense, once hate is gone, they will be forced to deal with pain."[3]

With some introspection, I see that underneath my anger toward Becca's situation is my own frailty, and underneath my fear of death is my being unable to protect my daughters from all that can happen to them in life. A car accident could take away both my ability to protect my daughters and my illusion that my best efforts will always protect them. Underneath my fear of death, I see the real pain of acknowledging my impotence to keep evil from happening to my beloved daughters. For as much as I would like to keep evil completely away from them, I don't have that ability. But I'd rather mask fear with one of the few emotions that men in our culture are allowed to express: anger.

We even drag Jesus into our attempt to validate our shallow emotion of anger. In the Gospels, there's a story of Jesus with whip in hand overturning tables of commerce that have been set up in the temple.

Jesus uses a whip to drive out the money changers who have turned a place of worship into a den of robbers. Some have made this story out to be Jesus inflicting physical harm on his enemies. A peculiar reading, in light of this being the same Jesus who commands his followers to turn the other cheek and who says about those who are killing him, "Father, forgive them," while dying on a cross. Instead of seeing Jesus overturning tables with a whip as a performance piece, in line with other Jewish prophetic acts such as Isaiah walking around naked and barefoot for three years and Hosea marrying a prostitute, we've turned the tables on this story, making it a prooftext of Jesus acting in anger—probably so we too can stay in the shallow emotion of anger.

Don't get me wrong, there's nothing wrong with being angry just as there's nothing wrong with eating baby food.

It's fine to eat baby food for a season when you are a baby, but it gets creepy when your coworker opens a jar of Gerber. Anger is a genuine and appropriate human response for a time and a season, but we must eventually excavate our soul to see what resides below.

Since anger is shallow, acting out of anger will always be easier.

Just like it's easier to fill yourself up on social media "friendships" instead of the genuine connections that don't happen on your terms and on your timelines.

Just like it's easier to spend thirty minutes on social media comparing your life to others' than it is to go for a walk or to do some yoga.

Just like it's easier to hustle at work where everyone looks up to you than to do the harder task of making things work at home with people who actually know you.

If we truly want to find our real issues, we don't stay in the shallows, because what resides in the shallows are symptoms. It's only when we move into the depths that we can find our monsters.

Into the Deep

FR. RICHARD ROHR once told me:

> The other Achilles' heel of Protestantism is that it has very little teaching on darkness and dryness. You have to go to the Catholic mystics for that. It's all about feelings and light. Not darkness. Without good teaching on darkness, you really think that the role of Christianity is to engage warm, fuzzy feelings. . . . You remember in the darkness what you once experienced in the light. Our word for that is faith. You hold on and then you realize that someone else is holding on to you.[4]

Fear keeps us standing in the shallows; love gets us to take a step. We faithfully step into the deep to befriend our monsters, often thinking that we are alone, only to realize we have never been alone because Someone is holding on to us. Love leads us past the shallow surface to what we don't know, so we can access new levels of our truest selves.

We've experienced isolation.

We've seen shallow connections.

We've felt anger.

All these originate in fear.

Love, the driving force of a benevolent Creator pushing creation forward, leads us beyond the shortsightedness of seeing into the mystery of unseeing.

To demonstrate this, let's go back to the story of the rich young ruler discussed in the previous chapter. Here's the same story but with a slightly different angle.

A young and wealthy politician approaches the popular new rabbi, hoping this rabbi will be one more person he can win over by his perfect image.

Beginning his performance, he says,

"Good Teacher, what must I do to be saved?"

The rabbi, sidestepping the subtle jab about being "good," answers with a traditional response to obey half of the Ten Commandments:

"Stay away from murder, adultery, theft, and lying, and honor your parents."

The politician smirks. "Teacher, I've kept all of these since my youth."

With love in his eyes, the rabbi looks past the young and wealthy politician's pompous grin to see the hurt within his soul.

"You are still missing one thing; sell everything you own and give the money to the poor."

On hearing these words, the smirk fades and the young and wealthy politician walks away.

This conversation was intended to be another opportunity for his ego to be stroked, but Rabbi Jesus invited him into the place where egos don't survive—the soul's deep recesses. Jesus didn't react to the smug, self-aggrandizing ploy to brag about his faithful obedience to the commandments. Jesus responded with a call to sell all he owns, not because Jesus wanted to hurt him but because Jesus loved him.

"Jesus, looking at him, *loved him* and said . . ."[5]

How often have *you* watched a selfish and greedy person hoard their resources and take when they should give, and felt love for them?

Okay, how about not love the selfish person but even like them?

How often have you looked at someone who was "so humbled" to post about every good deed they've ever done while being two WWJD bracelets above the legal limit and even thought, *I like them*?

Rarely if ever does that happen because we see the off-putting habits and want nothing to do with them. But Jesus "loved him" because Jesus sees beyond the visible habits to the subterranean hurt.

We see the symptoms and the habits that come from inner wounds, but Jesus, being God incarnate, never simply sees the outward appearance; Jesus sees the heart. Jesus knew who the rich young ruler was intended to be. The habits of greedy living and religious boasting were not part of the Creator's original design for him but rather the effects of the Monster of More wreaking havoc on his soul.

The reason we can go to our epistemic limits is because God looks beyond our symptoms, both our endearing performances and the off-putting ones, and loves us. The trust we have in God's ever-present love enables us to access what's beyond the limits of our comfort and our current level of knowing.

Love Heals

THE RICH YOUNG RULER'S MONSTERS motivated him to move, but unfortunately the movements were shallow. Greed is shallow. Begging for approval is shallow. God's intention for him, as it is for all of us, is the depth that love invites us into. As Scripture says, "God is love, and those who abide in love abide in God, and God abides in them" (1 John 4:16).

God is love. Love is God. Love is what pulls us forward. Fear is what holds us back.

When we make decisions based on greed, anger, lust, pride, self-righteousness, and others, which disfigure us, we are not abiding in love.

When we bravely move forward into our Creator's intent despite an unclear vision of all that entails, we are abiding in love. When we are moved to health and wholeness, it is love compelling us.

Fear makes you run away from the unknown.

Love makes you stay in the dark.

Fear says if others knew this about you, you'd be alone.

Fear says you will always be like this.

Fear says there's no way out.

Love says death has been swallowed up in victory.

Love says no matter what's unearthed, you will not be unfriended.

Love says no matter what you find and who you become, you will not be abandoned.

It has taken me some time, but I've come to accept Becca's wisdom. I'm learning to feel the anger, to accept it, but like my ER doctor, to treat it as a symptom of a deeper issue. This hasn't come naturally to me, but with intentionality we can develop the practice of looking below the surface to access those places beyond the limits of what's easily knowable.

Becca Stevens had every right to remain angry at God, the world, and the church after the assault she experienced, but she moved through anger to find healing for herself and for others. Becca started Thistle Farms, a diverse social enterprise with body and home products and a coffee shop that serves women coming out of prostitution and incarceration. She also founded Magdalene, Thistle Farms's residential community, which provides a two-year, rent-free place to live. Many women who eventually became sex workers or addicts were first victims of sexual assault. Becca now employs more than eighteen hundred women worldwide through Thistle Farms Global and has helped in the creation of forty sister communities nationally because she didn't stay shallow in anger. She moved to depth and experienced how love heals.

Love can do the same for you.

Go where you don't want to go, beyond the shallow symptoms, and what you will find is your monster. But you will also find the loving God who was drawing you there. You will find God's desire for you to no longer be conformed to the image that fear has contorted you into, but to be transformed by the healing power of love.

10

What (Not) to Expect about Your Monster

Silver Bullet

IN FRENCH FOLKLORE, the Beast of Gevaudan attacked two hundred people across the countryside under the light of the moon. Many tactics to stop the wolf monster failed until a hunter shot the beast with a silver bullet. Silver was recognized as the symbol for the moon, and the moon was recognized as the source of the Beast of Gevaudan's strength. What many previous attempts had failed to do, one bullet, forged out of the source of the wolf monster's strength, achieved.

Silver bullet mythology eventually became associated not just with this wolf monster but also with werewolves. A full moon shape-shifts a werewolf from presenting as a normal person into a violent beast. While in the werewolf state, only a silver bullet could stop the monster.

Silver bullet mythology says that with the right singular tactic your monstrous problem will be solved once and for all. I like this one-shot-solves-the-problem silver bullet mythology.

Or at least I used to.

In my college years, I had a beloved friend whom I desperately wanted to experience the life-changing good news of Jesus. I prayed and prayed for a way for him to encounter Jesus, but for him questions of spirituality and religion never surpassed the importance of questions regarding the next party's location or what he would be imbibing there.

A local church was having a special Easter service at which a couple would share their miraculous testimony of the husband's voice being restored after a disease had taken it away.

Here's the kicker: this miracle was recorded. So they wouldn't just talk about his voice being miraculously restored; they would play the audio tape of the miracle occurring. I just knew this would be the singular event that could change my friend because when have God's people ever witnessed a miracle and then quickly reverted to grumbling and complaining in unfaithfulness?

Well, not counting the Israelites' unfaithfulness despite experiencing the exodus from Egypt's ten plagues and walking through the Red Sea on dry land. And also not counting basically everyone who witnessed Jesus's miracles who still scattered by the time Jesus went to the cross.

After much negotiation, we came to a deal in which both of us would do what neither of us had done during college: he would attend a church service for one hour and I would drink two beers with him.

I assumed if I got him to the service, the account of the miracle would indelibly change him, making him forever abstain from any alcohol, even if Jesus himself made it, and thus I wouldn't have to corrupt my soul by imbibing the devil's juice.

I meet my friend in the church parking lot. Despite the Easter Sunday crowd, it is easy to find him as he is the only one smelling like a Bob Marley concert. Just as the music begins, we find two seats at the end of the eighth row, close enough for him to get a contact high from the miracle. The music goes on for a solid half hour, which isn't how I would have allocated half of the Lord's custody time, but I wasn't worried yet.

At the thirty-minute mark, the pastor introduces the couple, which takes ten minutes because preachers never believe in brevity.

Now I'm starting to sweat because I have only twenty minutes left and the miracle couple is going on and on about the Bible.

"Hey, we didn't come to this service to hear about the Bible; we came to hear the tape!" I want to shout. But I stay seated and my friend checks his watch.

At the fifty-eight-minute mark, they finally begin to play the tape of the miracle. A classic buzzer beater. God waits until the last minute, and now it's about to happen.

The tape plays and the man is reading from Psalm 103 (NIV),

"Praise the LORD, my soul; all my inmost being . . ."

Now I'm confused. I can hear the man whose voice was supposedly restored. Sure, his voice sounds like the whispers of an old man who's been smoking a carton of Marlboros every week since he was six, but he's still talking. How can his voice be restored, if he still has the ability to talk?

As I'm pondering the showmanship of this miracle, he continues reading Scripture.

"Who forgives all your sins and heals all your diseases."

And the change happens. It's like if you were streaming a show with weak internet. The show constantly stops to buffer, and when it plays, the picture is grainy and blurry. Then your internet instantly switches to high speed, making the picture crystal clear.

His gravelly smoker's voice disappears, and he speaks clearly.

I wouldn't score the miracle a perfect 10 but a solid 5. It's like the peanut butter and jelly sandwich of miracles. It's no Michelin restaurant meal, but it's still capable of getting the job done.

And to be clear, the job to get done was to cause someone who was not interested in following Jesus to have a Saul-of-Tarsus-road-to-Damascus-type conversion.

I don't stare at my friend but play it cool, knowing that by now he will be sobbing uncontrollably, eagerly waiting to confess all his sins.

A minute later, I casually glance over at him. He is unfazed.

We lock eyes and he raises his watch, showing me that it's five minutes beyond the agreed-upon time. I nod my head. We shake hands. He stands up and walks out, and I slump into my chair, dejected, as the ineffective silver bullet falls to the ground.

For werewolves, silver bullets work great but rarely for the rest of us. But that doesn't stop many of us from still believing that this new prayer technique or that new book or this new church or that renewed dedication to practicing willpower will eradicate our monsters once and for all.

We end up dejected because monsters always come back.

Anthropologist David Gilmore writes:

> The typical story of attack shows a recurrent structure, no matter what the culture or setting. As (Joseph) Campbell and many other students of myth have discovered, the story is basically threefold, a repetitive cycle. First, the monster mysteriously appears from shadows into a placid unsuspecting world, with reports first being disbelieved, discounted, explained away, or ignored. Then there is depredation and destruction, causing an awakening. Finally, the community reacts, unites, and, gathering its forces under a hero-saint, confronts the beast. Great rejoicing follows, normalcy returns. Temporarily thwarted by this setback, the monster (or its kin) returns at a later time, and the cycle repeats itself. Formulaic and predictable, the dialectic is predictable to the point of ritualism.[1]

Monster appears, monster destroys, then monster gets defeated.

I'll bet you've experienced victorious seasons over your anxieties and compulsions when the fear seemed to have been vanquished, enabling peace to pervade. But then, out of nowhere, your monster's ugly head reappeared. The first few times the monster returned, you were in disbelief because you felt that you had vanquished the monster. So you reassessed your techniques and decided you hadn't actually used the correct silver bullet. You redoubled your defense with a slightly different plan, yet the same cycle repeated itself. There was a brief season of peace, then the monster returned. Then disillusionment finally set in and the hope of the silver bullet mythology died out.

False Advertising

RED BULL, THE ENERGY DRINK COMPANY, had to change their tagline from "Red Bull gives you wings" to "Red Bull gives you wiiings" after settling a class-action lawsuit for thirteen million dollars because on further inspection, the drink doesn't actually give you wings.

Whether it's an energy drink that doesn't cause appendages to sprout, yogurt that isn't "scientifically proven" to boost your immune system, cars that aren't low-emission, or shoes that don't make your hindquarters shape up, no one likes false advertising.[2]

One can only imagine the type of false advertising lawsuits that could be filed against modern spiritual teachers over their ubiquitous claims of vanquishing issues for good by following their methods. The apostle Paul, on the other hand, never pretended to have access to such a silver bullet. Paul even writes the church in Corinth of his failed attempt to remove his monster, telling them that he repeatedly begged God to remove "a thorn" from his side, yet it never departed.

> Three times I appealed to the Lord about this, that it would leave me, but he said to me, "My grace is sufficient for you, for power is made perfect in weakness." (2 Cor. 12:8–9)

If the apostle Paul couldn't convince God to remove his monsters, maybe we shouldn't expect ours to be eradicated either. That doesn't mean there can't be improvement in learning how to deal with the monster, making the pull less effective. It might be more manageable, it might look and feel different, even though the pull still exists.

So we must not be deceived about our ability to vanquish our monsters forever; instead, we must befriend them.

Paul prayed for the absence of a thorn but what he received was the presence of a grace that made the thorn bearable. Similarly for us, salvation rarely looks like the absence of the dark pull; instead, salvation is experienced in the presence of a glimmer of light, encouraging us to keep going. It's the sliver of light sneaking under the closed door to give you just enough awareness to know where to place your next step in the darkened room. Deliverance rarely means the absence of the dark presence but rather an awareness of the presence of the light.

In regard to her expectations of what faith would do for her when she began reengaging with church, Brené Brown said:

> I went back to church thinking that it would be like an epidural, like it would take the pain away . . . that church would make the pain go away. Faith and church was not an epidural for me at all; it was like a midwife who just stood next to me saying, "Push. It's supposed to hurt a little bit."[3]

Faith doesn't rid us of the painful thorn, but faith does give us the presence of the graceful voice that keeps us moving one step at a time. Faith doesn't get rid of the monsters in our closets, but it gives us the grace and courage to befriend them daily. For our sanity, we must avoid fantasy at all cost, including the fantastical expectation that our monster will ever be gone once and for all. For those still holding to the false advertisement of the silver bullet mythology, there's an extra step required for befriending our monsters: we must first mourn the loss of the silver bullet.

We mourn that we will never fully eradicate the temptation to parrot the voices all around us.

We mourn that we will never get enough stuff to fill our cracked souls.

We mourn the continued presence of the voice tempting us to identify ourselves with our successes or failures.

Healthy mourning might look like forgiving the parent who gave you the predisposition to this issue, the spouse who helped the monster flourish in your soul, or the boss who manipulated your monster to get you to do what they wanted you to do.

Maybe healthy mourning requires you to forgive yourself.

Maybe it even includes forgiving God, who hasn't removed your monster.

Maybe it requires you to stop idolizing a relationship by expecting that person to fix the lack within your soul. Some people are resentful of a disappointing relationship, not because they think so little of the person but because they've unrealistically elevated the person to a divine level that no person can fulfill.

Once you've started the mourning process, you can move forward because a realistic way to befriend your monster exists. The way might not be enough to get rid of the monster once and for all, but it is enough to sustain you one day at a time.

One by One

A FEW YEARS INTO OUR CHURCH PLANT, I preached on Augustine's metaphor of sin curving us inward on ourselves, saying,

"God intends for us to not have a posture toward the world that's been closed off by timidity or fear but to have an open-handed, arms-spread-wide posture to all of the world, just as Jesus did when hanging on the cross. Yet the pull of darkness closes us in on ourselves like years of arthritis can shrivel a hand into a perpetually clenched fist.

The redemptive work of God's grace can undo the effect of sin like a physical therapist opening a patient's arthritic hand." I then went into detail describing how a physical therapist pulls open a patient's arthritic, clenched hand while acting the process out in the typical dramatic preacher style.

Maybe *detail* isn't the right word because I didn't technically do any research on how a therapist actually would open a hand. I didn't even take two minutes to do a cursory Google search; instead, I trusted in my preacher's poetic license.

So, yes, technically speaking I just made it up.

Which felt fine until after the service ended and I was called over to talk with someone who had both a medical license and personal experience.

Two decades earlier, Craig was a husband, a father, and a physician in his early thirties when he received the news that he had multiple sclerosis.

Today, his boys are both in medical school, and he's in a wheelchair with his clenched fists placed across each other in his lap. Every Sunday, his wife or a friend places the sacraments in his mouth as his arms can no longer hold the bread or the cup.

"Luke, grab my hand," Craig says after he called me over.

"What?" I reply.

"Grab my left hand," Craig repeats.

I sheepishly pull his frail left arm from across his lap and extend his arm toward me.

"Try to open my hand."

I make a halfhearted attempt to open his closed fist with no movement from his fingers.

"Harder," he says.

Now I'm in a conundrum. Do I rudely ignore his request to pull on his hand, or do I pull with such force as to possibly hurt my friend? To add another layer, his wife is an elder of our church. The last thing I want is to have to go to an elders' meeting after having broken the hand of an elder's spouse.

I slightly increase my force but still make no movement toward opening the clenched fist of a man who weighs half as much as I do.

"Now try opening just one finger," Craig says.

I gently grab his index finger and it easily extends.

"Grab another finger."

I grab the middle finger, and it glides open.

"And another."

I then pull open his ring finger, then his pinkie, then finally his thumb. And now his hand is fully open.

"Luke, my physical therapist does open my hand, but it's always one finger at a time."

Grace opens us up but rarely all at once.

We are saved in an instant but delivered incrementally.

We crave silver bullets, but what we receive are the practices of opening ourselves up one day at a time.

This is how God usually works. When the Israelites wandered in the wilderness, God provided food but not by sending them a lifetime supply. Instead, it was the daily raining down of manna. The food wasn't enough for a year, a month, or even a week. It was just enough for one day. The Israelites initially tried to store it up, but the saved food rotted. God didn't want them to have a lifetime supply of bread, only daily bread. Just as Jesus teaches us to pray, "Give us this day our daily bread."

The bread that God sent the Israelites was called *manna*, which in Hebrew literally means, "What is it?" The graces that God rains down on us can also cause us to ask, "What is this?" because grace rarely works according to our expectations and timelines. But that doesn't mean grace isn't at work.

Grace rarely gets rid of the monster once and for all, but grace is enough to sustain you one day at a time.

Practices

MAX BEERBOHM'S SHORT STORY *The Happy Hypocrite: A Fairy Tale for Tired Men* tells the story of Lord George Heaven, a man who lived a life marked by greed, superficial relationships, and alcohol abuse.[4] One evening while out with his current girlfriend, George sees a beautiful, wholesome woman. George is immediately smitten and desperately wants to marry her, but he can't because she has vowed only to marry a man with the face of a saint.

George has no face of a saint, so he acquires one at a mask shop. With his new saintly appearance, George wins the woman's heart and proposes marriage, and she accepts.

That moment marks the beginning of a moral conversion in George. He signs the wedding certificate not as Lord George but as George Heaven. He donates money to the poor, repays everyone he has cheated, and becomes humble before people whom he had never noticed before. George enters the life of a saint.

Some time later, George's ex-girlfriend sees him in his new appearance out for dinner with his new wife. The ex decides to rip the mask off George's face to expose his true identity. She successfully attacks him and knocks the mask to the ground. She laughs in triumph. Terrified, George looks to his wife, revealing his true face for the first time.

George is shocked when she asks him why he had a mask created that looks precisely like his own countenance.

When George entered the way of a saint, an unknown and unseen power began to change him. As he went about living the life of a saint, he took on the appearance of a saint.

This is the power of grace. The cumulative effect of daily saintly decisions reorients our faces into the face we were created to have. It doesn't happen with one simple act, but over time the power of habit can change our countenance. The fourth-century church leader Saint Basil of Caesarea says that "God grants us the divine image in our birth, but it is only via active choices and free will that we come to resemble the likeness of God."[5]

N. T. Wright describes the cumulative effect of daily decisions with the word *virtue*.

> Virtue, in this sense, isn't simply another way of saying "goodness." The word has sometimes been flattened out like that (perhaps we instinctively want to escape its challenge), but that isn't its strict meaning. Virtue, in this strict sense, is what happens when someone has made a thousand small choices, requiring effort and concentration, to do something which is good and right but which doesn't "come naturally"—and then on the thousand and first time, when it really matters, they find that they do what's required "automatically," as we say.[6]

Wright illustrates his concept of virtue with the story of pilot Chesley Sullenberger III, aka Captain Sully. On January 15, 2009, two minutes into flight 1549 from New York's LaGuardia Airport to Charlotte, Captain Sully's plane flew into a flock of Canada geese, disabling both engines.* Sully glided the now-powerless plane to the Hudson River where he landed it without injury to any of the 150 passengers, earning the landing the moniker "The Miracle on the Hudson."

But was it a miracle?

Well, Sully was flying at five hundred miles per hour in the sky in a metal tube that he landed† safely on a river. So yes, it was miraculous in the general sense.

But was it really a miracle?

I'm not so sure. It would truly be a miracle if I had landed the plane, as I have never made one choice that would enable me to land a plane anywhere, especially not on a river.

But Sully didn't just make one choice, he had made a lifetime of choices.

As a sixteen-year-old living in Denison, Texas, he chose to learn how to fly a single-engine light airplane.

He then chose to attend the United States Air Force Academy.

He then chose to become a pilot in the Air Force.

He then chose to spend three decades as a commercial pilot.

He also chose to earn a plethora of certifications, including a pilot certification in gliders.

What happened wasn't a singular, miraculous momentary decision, disconnected from the entirety of his life, but the culmination of a series of choices. That's the formative power of virtue.

---

*One can assume the geese were Canadian because their last words were "Sorry, eh."

†Or um . . . watered?

Paul writes in 2 Corinthians 3:18, "And all of us, with unveiled faces, seeing the glory of the Lord as though reflected in a mirror, are being transformed into the same image from one degree of glory to another; for this comes from the Lord, the Spirit."

The image we are transformed into, the divine likeness, happens one degree of likeness at a time. It's not a once-for-all change but the slow, steady change that happens one day and one moment at a time. Followers of Jesus are called *disciples* because the practice of following Jesus requires the daily disciplines of carrying our own crosses and denying ourselves. These daily decisions enable us to eventually reap the harvest of not only our likeness being transformed but also our monsters being transformed from terrors that haunt us into warnings that save us.

Accept that grace rarely gets rid of the monsters once for all, but trust that grace is enough to sustain you one day at a time.

A Final Blessing

SADLY, THIS BOOK HASN'T OFFERED YOU a silver bullet, despite how much I wish I had access to a silver bullet for both your sake and mine. I hope this book has instead pointed you to an unseen power at work within you, shaping you into a truer picture of who you were created to be. My prayer for you is that you would follow its leading.

Miroslav Volf once said:

> Prayer is a prayer into the darkness. This ability to step into the darkness is absolutely essential. Then clarity and the light comes after I've been in the darkness.
>
> That's what faith is.

Faith not in seeing things.

But faith in unseeing.[7]

May you face the darkness, trusting that not only your fears reside in the unknown but also the unseen power of love and grace.

May you trust in the life-changing power of love and grace.

May you believe that love and grace are just as real as fear and shame.

May you believe that the unseen power leads you toward life even if all you currently feel is death.

May you take captive all negative thoughts and make them obedient to love.

May you be blessed with a holy dissatisfaction with surface solutions.

Don't just see with the mechanism by which you cope; address the pain that causes your desire to cope.

Don't just feel the need to armor yourself with an appearance of having it all together; address your inability to accept your own flawed self.

Don't just acknowledge the anger that causes your condescension of others; address your self-condemnation.

Don't just name your unhealthy relationship with power and control; address your fear of vulnerability.

And most of all, may you trust that what you initially saw as monsters intended to destroy you were actually invitations used by your loving heavenly parent to save you.

Acknowledgments

To MY THOUGHTFUL and talented and beloved friends in the *Two Men and a Lady and the World's Last True Family Man* group text—Annie F., Jonathan Merritt, and Jason Miller. It's been an honor to mentor all of you.

To those who got me writing by reading lots of terrible stuff—Wade Hodges and Mikel Faulkner.

Thanks to Josh Graves, Josh Ross, Jonathan Storment, Chris Seidman, Rick Atchley, Randy Harris, and Mike Cope. And also The Intern, Honesty Mary's, Danielle Hejl, and sharks.

Thanks to my dear friend Richard Beck, whose blog series about Monsters back in 2009 helped shape some of this concept. In a truly circle-of-life kind of way, my father was Richard's first psychology professor in college. So whatever I stole from Richard, he probably first stole from my father. But still, go buy some of Richard's books.

Thanks to my outstanding agent, Greg Daniel.

To the girl in my tenth grade English class who got annoyed whenever I used vocab words in normal class discussions—my proclivity toward linguistic erudition wouldn't exist without the animus my sophomoric attempts at humorous would elicit from you.

To all of you from the Venture Community and Westover Hills Church of Christ for helping me process this monstrous idea.

To all the podcast listeners and church parishioners and internet friends who've bravely shared their monsters with me—it is truly an honor to walk with you through the darkness.

To Gisèle Mix, Patti Brinks, Brian Thomason, and the rest of the team at Baker.

Most of all, to my family.

Avery, Adalyn, and Audrey, you have made my heart full.

Lindsay, the best is yet to come.

Notes

Chapter 1 Fake Monsters, Real Fears

1. André Leroi-Gourhan, *The Dawn of European Art: An Introduction to Paleolithic Cave Painting*, trans. Sara Champion (Cambridge: Cambridge University Press, 1982), 54–55.

2. David Gilmore, *Monsters: Evil Beings, Mythical Beasts, and All Manner of Imaginary Terrors* (Philadelphia: University of Pennsylvania Press, 2003), 12.

3. Alix Spiegel, "Mining Books to Map Emotions through a Century," NPR, April 1, 2013, https://www.npr.org/sections/health-shots/2013/04/01/17 5584297/mining-books-to-map-emotions-through-a-century.

4. Adam Hamilton, *Unafraid* (New York: Convergent, 2018), 4.

5. Hamilton, *Unafraid*, 5.

6. "Shame v. Guilt," *Brené Brown* (blog), January 14, 2013, https://brenebrown .com/blog/2013/01/14/shame-v-guilt/.

7. G. K. Chesterton has been attributed with the saying, but Chesterton didn't actually write this. It's a paraphrase of something he wrote in *Tremendous Trifles* that was misquoted from memory by Neil Gaiman at the beginning of *Coraline*.

8. Technically speaking, the word *monster* is from the Latin word *monstrum*, which itself is a derivative of the root word *monere*, which means "to warn." Stephen Asma, *On Monsters: An Unnatural History of Our Worst Fears* (New York: Oxford University Press, 2009), 12.

Chapter 2 Into the Dark

1. Blaise Pascal, GoodReads, accessed November 27, 2019, https://www.good reads.com/quotes/19682-all-of-humanity-s-problems-stem-from-man-s-inability-to-sit.

2. Adam Alter, *Irresistible: The Rise of Addictive Technology and the Business of Keeping Us Hooked* (New York: Penguin Books, 2006), 168.

3. Richard Beck, "The Theology of Calvin and Hobbes," *Experimental Theology*, September 28, 2008, http://experimentaltheology.blogspot.com/2008/09/theology-of-calvin-and-hobbes-part-3_28.html.

4. See 1 Pet. 3:19; 4:6.

5. Apostles' Creed, Loyola Press, accessed November 27, 2019, https://www.loyolapress.com/our-catholic-faith/prayer/traditional-catholic-prayers/prayers-every-catholic-should-know/apostles-creed, emphasis added.

6. Wikipedia, s.v. "Hero's journey," accessed November 27, 2019, https://en.wikipedia.org/wiki/Hero%27s_journey.

7. Barbara Brown Taylor, *Learning to Walk in the Dark* (New York: HarperOne, 2014), 5.

8. Neel Burton, "Jung: The Man and His Symbols," *Psychology Today*, updated June 21, 2019, https://www.psychologytoday.com/us/blog/hide-and-seek/201204/jung-the-man-and-his-symbols.

9. Frederick Buechner, *Beyond Words: Daily Readings in the ABC's of Faith* (New York: HarperCollins, 2004), 139.

Chapter 3 Destroy

1. Hannah Arendt, *Eichmann in Jerusalem: A Report on the Banality of Evil* (New York: Penguin Books, 2006), 278–79.

2. Cari Romm, "Rethinking One of Psychology's Most Infamous Experiments," *Atlantic*, January 28, 2015, https://www.theatlantic.com/health/archive/2015/01/rethinking-one-of-psychologys-most-infamous-experiments/384913/.

3. Michael Schmidt, "Investigator in Secret Service Prostitution Scandal Resigns," *New York Times*, October 28, 2014, https://www.nytimes.com/2014/10/29/us/politics/investigator-in-secret-service-prostitution-scandal-resigns-after-being-implicated-in-own-incident.html.

4. Leonard Cohen, "Anthem," track 5 on *The Future*, Columbia Records, 1992.

5. Matt Patches, "*Blackfish* Director Gabriela Cowperthwaite on Killer Whales and the 20th Anniversary of *Free Willy*," July 23, 2013, Vulture, https://www.vulture.com/2013/07/free-willy-sea-world.html.

6. Richard Rohr, *Things Hidden: Scripture as Spirituality* (Cincinnati: Franciscan Media, 2007), 25.

7. John Steinbeck, *East of Eden* (New York: Penguin, 2016), 413.

Chapter 4 Deliver

1. Steven Pressfield, "Writing a Great Villain," *Steven Pressfield* (blog), May 2017, https://stevenpressfield.com/2017/05/writing-a-great-villain/?mc_cid=d8aa9fe055&mc_eid=46955499da.

2. Pressfield, "Writing a Great Villain."

3. Philip Yancey, *What Good Is God? In Search of a Faith That Matters* (New York: Jericho, 2013), 240.

4. Carol Lee Flinders, *Enduring Grace: Living Portraits of Seven Women Mystics* (New York: HarperCollins, 1993), 111.

Section II The Three Universal Monsters

1. Henri Nouwen, "Being the Beloved," YouTube, 3:30, *Hour of Power*, 1992, https://www.youtube.com/watch?v=v8U4V4aaNWk.

Chapter 5 Comparison

1. Jonathan Haidt, *The Happiness Hypothesis: Finding Modern Truth in Ancient Wisdom* (New York: Basic Books, 2006), 100.

2. Alter, *Irresistible*, 217.

3. Quoted in Jon Tyson, *The Burden Is Light: Liberating Your Life from the Tyranny of Performance and Success* (New York: Multnomah, 2018), 32.

4. Alain de Botton, *Status Anxiety* (New York: Knopf, 2008), 8.

5. Henri Nouwen, *Life of the Beloved: Spiritual Living in a Secular World* (New York: Crossroads, 2002), 1.

6. Frans de Waal, "Two Monkeys Were Paid Unequally: Excerpt from Frans de Waal's TED Talk," YouTube, April 4, 2013, https://www.youtube.com/watch?v=meiU6TxysCg. Thanks to Jon Tyson for introducing me to this study in his outstanding book *The Burden Is Light*.

7. Walter Brueggemann, *Genesis: Interpretation: A Bible Commentary for Teaching and Preaching* (Atlanta: John Knox, 1982), 56–57.

8. See Heb. 11:4.

9. I discussed this subject matter in a sermon once. That evening while trying to go to sleep, not always an easy task for me on Sunday nights, my wife says as I'm dozing off, "I bet someone could think that you are saying that God is

okay with different races not being treated equally." And with that comment, in rolled a wave of shame keeping me wide awake for the next two hours. To be clear, God as revealed in Jesus shows the divine heart for all and the call for a need to work toward a more just future for all people, genders, races, and ethnicities. This point is referring to the differences in individuals' talents, not the unjust treatment of people groups. Long story short—don't be okay with racism.

10. Wade Hodges, "The Bag of Walnuts," wadehodges.com, November 11, 2013, http://www.wadehodges.com/the-bag-of-walnuts/. The original story comes from Nasrudin.

11. John 21:22.

12. Martin Buber, *Tales of the Hasidim: The Early Masters* (New York: Schocken Books, 1947), 236–37.

Chapter 6 More

1. Shel Silverstein, *Where the Sidewalk Ends* (New York: HarperCollins, 1974), 160–61.

2. *Jurassic Park*, directed by Steven Spielberg (Universal City, CA: Universal Studios, 1993).

3. Haidt, *The Happiness Hypothesis*, 84–85.

4. Judg. 11:39.

5. Ronald Rolheiser, *Wrestling with God: Finding Hope and Meaning in Our Daily Struggles to Be Human* (New York: Image, 2018), 56.

6. Quoted in Andrés Claro, "Broken Vessels: Philosophical Implications of Poetic Translation," *The New Centennial Review* 9, no. 3 (Winter 2009): 95–136, https://muse.jhu.edu/search?action=search&query=content:Andr%C3%A9s%20Claro.%20%E2%80%9CBroken%20Vessels%7C%, accessed May 31, 2018.

7. Daniel Gilbert, *Stumbling on Happiness* (New York: Random House, 2006), 241.

8. Brené Brown, "Brené Brown on joy and gratitude," YouTube video, 3:42, November 28, 2012, https://www.youtube.com/watch?v=2IjSHUc7TXM.

Chapter 7 Success

1. In Matthew's account (20:21), James and John's mom asked. In Mark's account (10:35), the brothers asked.

2. Scott Cacciola, "J.J. Redick, the N.B.A's. Most Meticulous Player," *New York Times*, March 21, 2018, https://www.nytimes.com/2018/03/21/sports/jj-redick-sixers.html.

3. "James Corden on Pre-Performance Rituals, American Sports Fandom, and Musical Comedy," *The JJ Redick Podcast*, December 6, 2017, 14:30, https://podbay.fm/podcast/1317853625/e/1512584996.

4. Richard Beck, *The Slavery of Death* (Eugene, OR: Cascade Books, 2013), 60.

5. Eugene Peterson, *Christ Plays in Ten Thousand Places: A Conversation in Spiritual Theology* (Grand Rapids: Eerdmans, 2005), 117.

6. Charles Dickens, *A Christmas Carol*, Bantam Classic (New York: Bantam Books, 2009), 17, emphasis added.

7. "Richard Rohr: The Divine Dance (Part 1)," *Newsworthy with Norsworthy* (podcast), September 19, 2016, 18:35, https://player.fm/series/newsworthy-with-norsworthy-2360242/richard-rohr-the-divine-dance-part-1.

8. Warren Buffett, "My Philanthropic Pledge," *Fortune*, June 16, 2010, http://archive.fortune.com/2010/06/15/news/newsmakers/Warren_Buffett_Pledge_Letter.fortune/index.htm.

9. Leonard Mlodinow, *The Drunkard's Walk: How Randomness Rules Our Lives* (New York: Vintage Books, 2009), 195.

10. Job 38:3.

Section III A Monster-Friendly Life

1. Parker Palmer, *The Active Life: A Spirituality of Work, Creativity, and Caring* (San Francisco: Jossey-Bass, 1990), 31.

Chapter 8 How (Not) to Dress for Your Monster

1. Friedrich Nietzsche, *Beyond Good and Evil*, trans. R. J. Hollingdale (New York: Penguin Books, 2003), part 4, no. 146.

2. Gerald Corey, *Theory and Practice of Counseling and Psychotherapy*, seventh ed. (Belmont, CA: Brooks/Cole, 2005), chap. 5.

3. Richard Rohr, *The Immortal Diamond: The Search for Our True Self* (San Fransisco: Jossey-Bass, 2013), 36.

4. Mark 10:21.

5. Asma, *On Monsters*, 12.

6. For more on Paul's zeal and righteousness, see N. T. Wright, *Paul: A Biography* (New York: HarperOne, 2018).

7. Janet G. Woititz, *Adult Children of Alcoholics*, exp. ed. (Deerfield Beach, FL: Health Communications, 1983).

8. Rolheiser, *Wrestling with God*, 34.

Chapter 9 Where (Not) to Find Your Monster

1. M. Scott Peck, *People of the Lie: The Hope for Healing Human Evil* (New York: Touchstone, 1998), 32.

2. "Becca Stevens: Love Heals," *Newsworthy with Norsworthy* (podcast), October 22, 2017, 19:30, https://lukenorsworthy.com/2017/10/23/becca-stevens -love-heals/.

3. James Baldwin, *The Fire Next Time* (New York: Vintage Books, 1993), https://www.goodreads.com/quotes/1867-i-imagine-one-of-the-reasons -people-cling-to-their.

4. "Richard Rohr: The Universal Christ (Part 2)," *Newsworthy with Norsworthy* (podcast), March 18, 2019, 1:03, https://lukenorsworthy.com/2019/03/18 /richard-rohr-the-universal-christ-part-2/.

5. Mark 10:21, emphasis added.

Chapter 10 What (Not) to Expect about Your Monster

1. Gilmore, *Monsters*, 13.

2. Julien Rath, "18 False Advertising Scandals That Cost Some Brands Millions," Business Insider, February 27, 2017, http://www.businessinsider.com /false-advertising-scandals-2017-2#red-bull-said-it-could-give-you-wings-6.

3. Brené Brown, "Jesus Wept," The Work of the People, March 19, 2016, 5:44, https://www.facebook.com/theworkofthepeople/videos/10154011327415 682/.

4. Max Beerbohm, *The Happy Hypocrite: A Fairy Tale for Tired Men* (Create-Space Independent Publishing, 2015).

5. Quoted in Craig Detweiler, *Selfies: Searching for the Image of God in a Digital Age* (Grand Rapids: Brazos, 2018), 73.

6. N. T. Wright, *After You Believe: Why Christian Character Matters* (New York: HarperCollins, 2010), 20.

7. "Miroslav Volf: For the Life of the World," *Newsworthy with Norsworthy* (podcast), March 25, 2019, 33:00, https://lukenorsworthy.com/2019/03 /25/miroslav-volf-for-the-life-of-the-world/. The quote was said in the context of Paul's words in Romans 8 on not knowing how to pray.

Luke Norsworthy (MDiv, Abilene Christian University) is the senior minister of the Westover Hills Church of Christ in Austin, Texas. He is the author of *God over Good* and the host of the popular *Newsworthy with Norsworthy* podcast on which he has rubbed shoulders with some of the brightest and most prominent voices in theology. He lives in Austin, Texas, with his wife and three daughters.

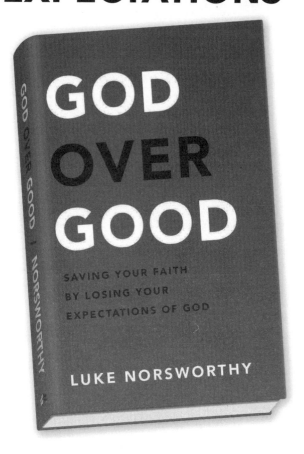
 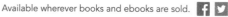

GET CONNECTED
WITH LUKE!

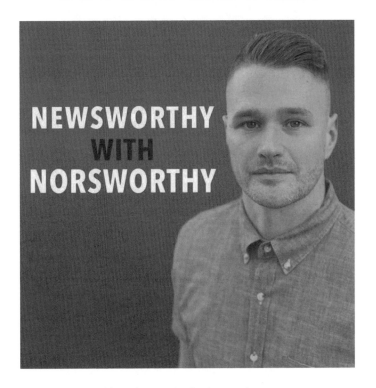

Check out Luke's podcast
Newsworthy with Norsworthy, a weekly
discussion on spirituality, Christianity, and
anything else that is newsworthy.

**Listen now at LukeNorsworthy.com
or wherever you tune in to podcasts!**

 LukeNors

LukeNorsworthy

 NewsworthywithNorsworthy

LIKE THIS
BOOK?
Consider sharing it with others!

- Share or mention the book on your social media platforms. Use the hashtag **#BefriendingYourMonsters**.

- Write a book review on your blog or on a retailer site.

- Pick up a copy for friends, family, or anyone who you think would enjoy and be challenged by its message!

- Share this message on Twitter, Facebook, or Instagram: I loved **#BefriendingYourMonsters** by **@LukeNorsworthy @ReadBakerBooks**

- Recommend this book for your church, workplace, book club, or class.

- Follow Baker Books on social media and tell us what you like.

 ReadBakerBooks

 ReadBakerBooks

ReadBakerBooks